THE DIGBY PLAY OF
MARY MAGDALENE

THE DIGBY PLAY OF
MARY MAGDALENE

a *Broadview Anthology of Medieval Drama* edition

Contributing Editor,
The Digby Play of Mary Magdalene:
Chester N. Scoville, University of Toronto

General Editors,
The Broadview Anthology of Medieval Drama:
Christina M. Fitzgerald, University of Toledo
John T. Sebastian, Loyola Marymount University

broadview press

BROADVIEW PRESS – www.broadviewpress.com
Peterborough, Ontario, Canada

Founded in 1985, Broadview Press remains a wholly independent publishing house. Broadview's focus is on academic publishing; our titles are accessible to university and college students as well as scholars and general readers. With over 600 titles in print, Broadview has become a leading international publisher in the humanities, with world-wide distribution. Broadview is committed to environmentally responsible publishing and fair business practices.

How to cite this book: Broadview Anthology editions are stand-alone volumes presenting material that is also available within the stated anthology. Taken as a whole, each of these anthologies is typically the result of a highly collaborative editorial process. Where a contributing editor for a stand-alone volume is identified, however, that individual has taken primary responsibility for editing the particular volume, and should be named in any citation of that volume. (For example, this book should be cited as "edited by Chester N. Scoville"; in citing this volume there is no need to reference the general editors of *The Broadview Anthology of Medieval Drama*.)

Library and Archives Canada Cataloguing in Publication

The Digby play of Mary Magdalene / contributing editor, The Digby play of Mary Magdalene: Chester N. Scoville, University of Toronto; general editors, The Broadview anthology of medieval drama: Christina M. Fitzgerald, University of Toledo, John T. Sebastian, Loyola Marymount University.

(A Broadview anthology of medieval drama edition)
Includes bibliographical references.
ISBN 978-1-55481-423-7 (softcover)

1. Mary Magdalene, Saint—Drama. I. Scoville, Chester N., (Chester Norman), 1968-, editor

PR1261.M36 2017   822'.2   C2017-906622-6

Broadview Press handles its own distribution in North America:
PO Box 1243, Peterborough, Ontario K9J 7H5, Canada
555 Riverwalk Parkway, Tonawanda, NY 14150, USA
Tel: (705) 743-8990; Fax: (705) 743-8353
email: customerservice@broadviewpress.com

Distribution is handled by Eurospan Group in the UK, Europe, Central Asia, Middle East, Africa, India, Southeast Asia, Central America, South America, and the Caribbean. Distribution is handled by Footprint Books in Australia and New Zealand.

Broadview Press acknowledges the financial support of the Government of Canada through the Canada Book Fund for our publishing activities.

Canada

Developmental Editor: Jennifer McCue
Cover Design: Lisa Brawn

PRINTED IN CANADA

Contents

Acknowledgments

I'd like to thank Christina Fitzgerald and John Sebastian for their encouragement and support in my editing of this text, and Jennifer McCue and Don LePan for their support as well. I am grateful also to the staff of Robarts Library at the University of Toronto, and to the good people at Records of Early English Drama, especially Alexandra F. Johnston, for their support over the years. Thanks especially to Kim Yates, who is and remains the person without whom I could do nothing.

Introduction

The Digby Play of Mary Magdalene

The Digby Play of *Mary Magdalene* is unrivalled among early English plays in its complexity. Incorporating over fifty speaking parts, running for over five hours (if modern performances are a reliable guide), and featuring major theatrical effects, the play is a striking example of the ambition of early English theatrical production. Like its much smaller manuscript companion, *The Conversion of Saint Paul*, the play of *Mary Magdalene* takes as its basis the popular form of a saint's life or *hagiography*; unlike *Paul*, this play does not recount a singular episode in the life of its saint but rather attempts a full narrative of all known material about her, both biblical and legendary. It also freely incorporates elements of allegory as seen in such plays as *Wisdom* and *The Castle of Perseverance*, making it arguably a kind of *summa* of the different forms of English medieval drama.

At the heart of the play is Mary Magdalene, a complex figure of significant popularity during the Middle Ages; among female saints, she was second only to the Virgin Mary in her cultural importance. Part of the character's complexity derives from her history: Mary Magdalene as medieval Christians thought of her is a composite of several discrete figures from the New Testament and elsewhere. "Mary called Magdalene" is noted in the gospels as one of the disciples who accompanied Jesus on his travels; she is also noted as a witness to his crucifixion, death, and resurrection. However, during the early Christian period and into the Middle Ages, other women in the gospels became conflated with this figure—women such as Mary of Bethany (sister of Martha and Lazarus), and the sinful woman who weeps over Jesus's feet in the house of Simon the Leper. Neither of these women are identified as Mary Magdalene in the biblical text, but they came to be thought of as the same person through interpretation. In later centuries, even more stories and characteristics came to be associated with Mary Magdalene. Perhaps as a result of an association with Mary of Egypt, her family began to be described as noble, even royal class, and legends grew of her supposed missionary travels around the Mediterranean after Jesus's Ascension, and heremitical time in the wilderness at the end of her life. These stories were gathered in such sources as Jacobus de Voragine's thirteenth-century compendium of saints' lives, *Legenda Aurea* [*The Golden Legend*]. The playwright was thus drawing on a rich and lengthy tradition in the portrayal of his heroine.

One of the most striking and well-known aspects of this composite Magdalene figure was the widespread depiction of her as a reformed prostitute (as Mary of Egypt had been). Like several other medieval sources, however, the Digby play does not depict her as such; instead, she is simply said to have fallen into a life of sin and dissipation after the death of her father, only to have been suddenly redeemed by repentance and Christ's mercy. The key biblical source for this latter event is Luke 8.2, which mentions that Jesus had cast seven devils out of her; like some other medieval texts, the play identifies these devils with the Seven Deadly Sins. This identification, furthermore, facilitates the incorporation of such other allegorical figures as the World and the Flesh into the play. More importantly, it facilitates the portrayal of Mary Magdalene as a person beset not merely by lechery but by all of the sins; her story thus becomes an even more compelling example of the power of God's mercy and forgiveness.

The world in which Mary Magdalene is depicted is plagued by competing tyrants, all of whom boast of their power and demand unquestioning loyalty. In the first 250 lines of the play, no fewer than four such figures address the audience in similar terms, declaring their magnificence and threatening their hearers with dire consequences in the event of disobedience. The emphasis on power and boasting pervades the play at all levels of society, from the Emperor down to the Shipman's Boy. Even Mary Magdalene's father Cyrus begins his introduction to the audience in similar terms.

Of the figures of power who crisscross the playing space, only one does not begin by boasting and threatening: Jesus. He enters silently, speaking only after being invited to dinner by Simon Leprous, and then beginning his speech with a gracious expression of thanks; he concludes this scene with a moral discourse that sets him apart from the power-centered speeches of the tyrants. This contrast clearly demarcates a difference between following Christ and following any of the other figures who compete for the heroine's (and the implied audience's) respect. As is typical of medieval biblical plays, the difference between sides is not merely a matter of taste or caprice; it is stark and morally qualitative. The conversion of the King and Queen of Marseilles in the second half of the play makes this contrast most evident: a tyrant of exactly the type that dominates the play's opening is turned to the worship of Jesus, not only through impressive shows of power but also through artful discourse and effective preaching.

The play's manuscript is a part of Bodleian Digby MS 133, a composite collection which also includes *The Conversion of Saint Paul*, *The Killing of the Children*, and an incomplete text of *Wisdom*, as well as assorted texts on early science and natural magic. The manuscript of *Mary Magdalene* is written on paper. Following the lead of Baker, Murphy, and Hall in their standard 1982 scholarly edition, scholars commonly date it from between 1515 and 1525, based both on the visible watermarks and on the handwriting used by the scribe. As Baker et al. note, the manuscript of *Mary Magdalene* shows numerous signs of haste in completion: stanzas are left incomplete and fragmentary, lines are quite possibly missing in several places, speech attributions and stage directions are sometimes confused and overwritten. The manuscript usually distinguishes visually between spoken text (written in black or brown ink), unspoken text such as speech attributions (written in brown or red ink), and stage directions (written in red ink), but is not entirely consistent in these or other matters. The text as we have it is almost certainly not one that was used for performance, but is rather a copy made for some other purpose; the fact that the scribe's final quatrain begs the indulgence of readers rather than of players or of an audience suggests that the copy may have been for private devotional purposes. That is, however, uncertain.

There is a good deal of complexity as well in the multiplicity of the play's stanzaic forms. For the most part, the play is written in doubled quatrains with the rhyme scheme *ababbcbc*, or in single quatrains with the rhyme scheme *abab*. There are, however, many other forms of stanza throughout the play, including tail-rhyming stanzas (e.g., *aaabcccb*), rhyme royal stanzas (*ababbcc*), and several other stanzaic forms of varying lengths. There are some isolated couplets, and a number of isolated lines both in English and in Latin.

While the play's use of these varied forms does not entirely follow regular thematic or dramaturgical patterns, it is roughly the case that bad or low-born characters tend towards irregular and tail-rhyming forms, while good or high-born characters tend to speak in more regular stanzas. Alliteration, which appears frequently in the play, is also especially notable in the rantings of the tyrants. Both the use of alliteration and the use of irregular stanzaic form—stylistic qualities very frequently associated with villainy in early English drama—reach something of a climax in *Mary Magdalene* (perhaps even a *reductio ad absurdum*) in the nonsensical doggerel of the pagan priest's boy at lines 1185–1201, which may be compared with the orderly and relatively unalliterative sermon of Mary Magdalene at lines 1481–1525. There are, however, exceptions to these tendencies throughout the text.

The play's production is perhaps the most demanding in all of medieval English drama: among other things, it calls for a set to burn down in a fire, a ship to travel around the playing space, a pagan idol and temple to come crashing to the ground, and Mary's soul to be elevated to Heaven, accompanied by angels. Like several other surviving East Anglian plays (such as *The Conversion of Saint Paul*, the N-Town *Mary Play*, and *The Castle of Perseverance*), this play was certainly meant to be played outdoors using a scaffold-and-platea staging technique. As with the others, this play has no certain records of specific performance associated with it, although John Coldewey (1975) has noted that records from Chelmsford in the early 1560s may indicate a performance there; the connection with that town is also suggested by the play's connection with the book collector Myles Blomefylde, who was resident there and whose initials appear in a later hand at the top of the play's first leaf. The exact details of these connections, however, remain something of a puzzle.

The text of this play and its appendices was prepared using the procedures set out in *The Broadview Anthology of Medieval Drama*, edited by Christina M. Fitzgerald and John T. Sebastian, using modern spelling for English words and regularized spelling for Latin words, with modern punctuation throughout. In preparing the text I consulted the facsimile by Baker and Murphy; the online facsimile at the Bodleian; the 19th-century edition by Furnivall; the standard scholarly edition by Baker, Murphy, and Hall; the student anthology edition by Bevington; and the student anthology edition by Cold-ewey. For the excerpts from Caxton in the appendices, I have added quotation marks to denote dialogue, for the ease of modern readers. I have followed these procedures, some of which are unusual in the presentation of medieval drama but are common in the presentation of Early Modern texts, because, as Fitzgerald and Sebastian note, the English texts herein fall within the beginning of the Early Modern English period by the reckoning of many linguists. Rather than give an impression of something like Chaucerian Middle English with its quite different pronunciations, the present edition falls on the side of modernizing, placing the text in line with its later theatrical cousins as most undergraduate students will encounter them.

In the case of obsolete words I have, when possible, used the head-word spelling of the *Oxford English Dictionary*. Where there is no *OED* heading, or, when occasionally necessary to maintain rhyme, I have retained the original spelling and provided a gloss. The annota-tions provided throughout the text are, like the modernized spelling and punctuation, intended to make the text as accessible as possible for modern undergraduate students. I have not added additional stage directions to the play; the manuscript has many of its own, however, and they are set off in italics and within parentheses. The speech at-tributions within the play are sometimes inconsistent in their naming conventions; for clarity and consistency I have translated characters' names into English and regularized them. Characters who are named but do not speak are listed in square brackets. In dividing the text into its eccentric stanzaic divisions, I have followed the lead of Baker, Murphy, and Hall (1982), and of Coldewey (1993).

The Digby Play of Mary Magdalene[1]

CHARACTERS[2]

Emperor	Envy
Scribe	[Sloth]
Provost	[Gluttony]
Messenger	Bad Angel
Cyrus	Good Angel
Lazarus	Sensuality
Mary Magdalene	Taverner
Martha	Simon Leprous
Messenger	Jesus
Herod	Disciples
Philosopher 1	[Devil 1]
Philosopher 2	Devil 2
Knight 1	Knight 3
Knight 2	[Knight 4]
Pilate	Jew
Sergeant 1	King
Sergeant 2	Queen
World	Devil
Flesh	Mary Jacobe
Devil	Mary Salome
Seven Deadly Sins:	Angel 1
Pride / Curiosity	Angel 2
Lechery	Peter
Covetise	John
Wrath	Heathen Priest

---

1   *Mary Magdalene*   The present text has been edited by Chester N. Scoville, based on the facsimile edited by Donald C. Baker and J.L. Murray (1976), and the facsimile available at the Early Manuscripts at Oxford University website. All modern editions have been consulted. Spelling and punctuation have been modernized in accordance with the practices of *The Broadview Anthology of Medieval Drama*. All stage directions are from the manuscript, and are shown in parentheses. Characters' names and speech attributions, which are inconsistent in the manuscript, have been regularized somewhat.

2   CHARACTERS   The names of characters who appear but do not speak are listed in square brackets.

Clerk   Knight 5
Raphael   [Prince]
Shipman   Priest
Boy

EMPEROR.   I command silence, in the pain of forfeiture,
 To all mine° audience present general!   *my*
 Of my most highest and mightiest volunty,°   *will*
 I will° it be known to all the world universal   *wish*
5 That of Heaven and Hell chief ruler am I,
 To whose magnificence none standeth equal;
 For I am sovereign of all sovereigns subjugal°   *subject*
 Unto mine empire, being incomparable
 Tiberius Caesar,[1] whose power is potential.°   *powerful*

10 I am the blood royal, most of sovereignty.
 Of all emperors and kings, my birth is best,
 And all regions obey my mighty volunty.
 Life, and limb, and goods all be at my request.
 So, of all sovereigns, my magnificence most mightiest
15 May not be a-gainsaid° of° friend nor of foe, *denied / by*
 But all abide judgment and rule of my list.°   *pleasure*
 All grace upon Earth from my goodness cometh fro,° *forth*
 And that brings all people in bliss so.

 For the most worthiest, will I rest in my seat.[2]

20 SCRIBE.   Sir, from your person groweth much grace.
 EMPEROR.   Now, for thine° answer, Belial[3] bless thy face. *your*
 Mickle° prosperity I gin° to purchase;   *much / begin*
 I am wounden° in wealth from all woe.   *protected*

 Hark thou, Provost, I give thee in commandment:
25 All your people preserve in peaceable possession.° *control*

---

1 *Tiberius Caesar* Roman emperor from 14 CE to 37 CE.
2 *For the most ... my seat* The MS contains many examples of such stranded lines and
 fragmentary stanzas.
3 *Belial* Name of a devil in Christian and Jewish tradition.

If any there be to my gods disobedient,
Dissever° those harlots° and make to me   *disperse / criminals*
    declaration
And I shall make all such to die,
Those preachers of Christ's incarnation.
PROVOST.   Lord of all lords, I shall give you information.   30
EMPEROR.   Lo, how all the world obeyeth my domination;
That person is not born that dare me disobey.

Scribe, I warn you, see that my laws
In all your parts° have due obeisance.°   *regions / respect*
Inquire and ask, each day that dawns,   35
If in my people be found any variance
Contrary to me in any chance,°   *way*
Or with° my golden gods grouch or groan.   *against*
I will mar such harlots with murder and mischance.

If any such remain, put them in reprieve,°   *prison*   40
And I shall you relieve.°   *reward*

SCRIBE.   It shall be done, lord, withouten° any   *without*
    let° or without doubt!   *hindrance*
EMPEROR.   Lord and lad to my law doth lout,°   *bow*
Is it not so? Say you all, with one shout!

(*Here answereth all the people at once: "Yea, my lord, yea!"*)

EMPEROR.   So, ye froward° folks, now am I pleased.   *unruly*   45
Set wine and spices to° my council full clear.   *for*
Now have I told you my heart, I am well pleased.
Now let us sit down, all, and make good cheer.

(*Here enter Cyrus, the father of Mary Magdalene.*)

CYRUS.   Emperor, and kings, and conquerors keen,°   *brave*
Earls, and barons, and knights that been bold,   50
Birds° in my bower,° so seemly to seen,°   *ladies / dwelling / see*
I command you at once my hests° to hold!   *commands*

THE DIGBY PLAY OF MARY MAGDALENE   17

Behold my person, glistering° in gold,   *shining*
Seemly beseen of all other men!¹
55 Cyrus is my name, by cliffs so cold;²
I command you all obedient to been!°   *be*

Whoso will not, in bale° I them bring,   *harm*
And knit such caitiffs° in knots of care!   *vile persons*
This Castle of Magdalene is at my wielding,°   *command*
60 With all the country both less and more,
And lord of Jerusalem. Who against me don° dare?   *does*
All Bethany at my bidding be;
I am set in solace from all sighing sore,
And so shall all my posterity:
65 Thus for to liven,° in rest and royalty.   *live*

I have here a son that is full true to me,³
No comelier creature of God's creation;
Two amiable daughters, full bright° of blee,°   *beautiful / face*
Full glorious to my sight, and full of delectation.°   *delight*
70 Lazarus, my son, in my respection;⁴
Here is Mary, full fair and full of femininity;
And Martha, full of beauty and of delicacy,
Full of womanly mirrors° and of benignity.   *archetypes*
They have fulfilled my heart with consolation.

75 Here is a collection of circumstance:⁵
To my cognition,° never such another   *knowledge*
As by demonstration knit in continence,⁶
Save° alonely° my lady, that was their mother.   *except / only*
Now, Lazarus, my son, which art their brother,
80 The lordship of Jerusalem I give thee after my decease;°   *death*
And Mary, this castle alonely and none other;

---

1   *Seemly beseen ... men!*   Well-regarded by all other men.
2   *Cyrus ... so cold*   The significance of this phrase is uncertain.
3   *full true to me*   The MS reads "to me full true."
4   *Lazarus ... respection*   Lazarus, my son, pay attention to me.
5   *collection of circumstance*   Complete state of affairs.
6   *As by ... continence*   Proven to be bound in moral purity. Cyrus's confident declaration
    of his daughters' chastity sets up the importance and unexpectedness of Mary Magda-
    lene's fall.

And Martha shall have Bethany, I say express.
These gifts I grant you, withouten less,

While that I am in good mind.

LAZARUS.   Most reverent father, I thank you heartily   85
Of your great kindness showed unto me.
Ye have granted such a livelihood worthy
Me to restrain from all necessity.
Now, good Lord (and° His will it be),   *if*
Grant me grace to live to thy pleasure,[1]   90
And against° them so to rule me   *according to*
That we may have joy withouten variance.

MARY MAGDALENE.   Thou God of peace and principal counsel,
More sweeter is thy name than honey by kind.°   *nature*
We thank you, father, for your gifts royal,   95
Out of pains of poverty us to unbind.
This is a preservative from straitness° we find,   *poverty*
From worldly labors to my comforting,
For this livelihood is able° for the daughter of a king,   *fitting*

This place of pleasure, the sooth° to say.   *truth*   100
MARTHA.   O ye good father of great degree,°   *rank*
Thus to depart with your riches,
Considering our lowliness and humility,
Us to save from worldly distress!
Ye show us points° of great gentleness,°   *examples / nobility* 105
So meekly° to maintain us to° your grace.°   *humbly / by / generosity*
High in Heaven advanced mote° you be   *may*
In bliss, to see that Lord's face
When ye shall hence pass!
CYRUS.   Now I rejoice with all my mights;   110
To enhance° my children, it was my delight.   *promote*
Now, wine and spices, ye gentle° knights,   *noble*
Unto these ladies of gentleness.

---

1   *to thy pleasure*   In a way that is pleasing to you.

(Here shall they be served with wine and spices.)

EMPEROR.   Sir Provost, and Scribe, judges of my realm,
115   My messenger I will send into far country
Unto my seat of Jerusalem:
Unto Herod, that regent there under me,
And unto Pilate, judges of the country;
Mine intent I will them teach.
120   Take heed, thou Provost, my precept° written be,   *command*
And say I command them, as they will be out wretch,[1]
If there be any in the country against my law doth preach,

Or against my gods any trouble tells,
That thus against my laws rebels,
125   As he is regent and in that realm dwells
And holdeth his crown of me by right,
If there be any harlots that against me make
replication,°   *complaint*
Or any muttering against me make with
malignation.°[2]   *malice*
PROVOST.   Sir, of all this they shall have information,
130   So to uphold your renown and right!

EMPEROR.   Now, Messenger, withouten tarrying,°   *lingering*
Have here gold unto thy fee.[3]
So bear these letters to Herod the king
And bid him make inquirance in every country,
135   As he is judge in that country being.
MESSENGER.   Sovereign, your errand, it shall be done
full ready°   *quickly*
In all the haste that I may.
For to fulfill your bidding
I will not spare,° neither by night nor by day.   *neglect*

(Here goeth the messenger toward Herod.)

---

1   *as they … wretch*   If they do not wish any unpleasantness.
2   *If there be … malignation*   The Emperor never follows this lengthy if-clause with a
then-clause.
3   *unto thy fee*   For your payment.

HEROD.[1]   In the wild, waning world, peace all at once!   140
No noise, I warn you, for grieving of me!
If you do, I shall hurl off your heads, by Mahound's[2] bones,
As I am true king to Mahound so free.
Help! Help! That I had a sword!
Fall down, ye faitors,° flat to the ground!   *frauds*   145
Heave off your hoods and hats, I command you all!
Stand bare-head, ye beggars! Who made you so bold?
I shall make you know your king royal!
Thus will I be obeyed through all the world,
And whoso° will not, he shall be had in hold,[3]   *whoever*   150
And so to be cast in° cares cold,   *into*
That worken° any wonder° against   *work / extraordinary thing*
   my magnificence.
Behold these rich rubies, red as any fire,
With the goodly green pearl full set about.
What king is worthy or equal to my power?   155
Or, in this world who is more had° in doubt°   *held / fear*
Than is the high name of Herod, King of Jerusalem,
Lord of Aleppo, Asia, and Tyre,
Of Hebron, Beersheba, and Bethlehem?[4]
All these been° under my governance.   *are*   160
Lo, all these I hold withouten reprobation.°   *legal objection*
No man is to me equal, save alonely the Emperor
Tiberius, as I have in provostication.[5]
How say the philosophers by° my rich reign?   *about*
Am not I the greatest governor?   165
Let me understand, what can ye sayn?°   *say*

PHILOSOPHER 1.   Sovereign, and° it please you,   *if*
   I will express:

---

1 *HEROD* Herod II, king of the Roman client state of Judea. He appears in the New Testament as an antagonist of Jesus, and is a common figure in medieval drama, representing
   the quintessential mad tyrant.
2 *Mahound* Common Middle English form of the name of Mohammed, the founder of
   Islam (570–632 CE); he was often depicted in the Middle Ages as an idol worshipped by
   non-Christians of any sort, including Jews such as Herod.
3 *had in hold* Held in prison.
4 *Lord of Aleppo ... Bethlehem* Herod names five cities in the Middle East, in and around
   Roman Judea. By "Asia," he may mean Asia Minor, i.e., modern-day Turkey.
5 *as I have in provostication* From whom I derive my authority.

Ye be the ruler of this region
And most worthy sovereign of nobleness
170   That ever in Judea bore domination.
But, sir, Scripture giveth information
And doth rehearse° it verily:°   *describe / truly*
That child shall remain of great renown,
And all the world of him should magnify:°   *speak praise*

175   *Et ambulabunt gentes in lumine tuo, et reges*
In splendore ortus tui.[1]

HEROD.   And what sayest thou?
PHILOSOPHER 2.   The same verifieth my book: as how,

As the Scripture doth me tell,
180   Of a mighty duke° shall rise and reign,   *leader*
Which shall reign and rule all Israel.
No king against his worthiness shall obtain,°   *prevail*
The which in prophecy hath great eloquence:

Non auferetur sceptrum de Juda et dux de
185   *Femore eius donec veniet qui mittendus est.*[2]

HEROD.   Ah! Out! Out! Now am I grieved all with the worst!
Ye dastards!° Ye dogs! The Devil mote you draw![3]   *villains*
With flaying flaps I bid you to a feast![4]
A sword! A sword! These lurdans were slew![5]
190   Ye longbones! Losels!° Forsake ye that word!   *villains*
That caitiff shall be caught, and sure I shall him flay!
For him, many more shall be marred with murder!

---

1   *Et ambulabunt ... ortus tui* Latin: And the Gentiles shall walk in thy light, and kings in
     the brightness of thy rising (Isaiah 60.3).
2   *Non auferetur ... mittendus est* Latin: The scepter shall not be taken away from Juda,
     nor a ruler from his thigh, till he come that is to be sent (Genesis 49.10). A more modern
     biblical translation (NRSV) reads, "The scepter shall not depart from Judah, nor the
     ruler's staff from between his feet."
3   *The Devil mote you draw* May the Devil tear you to pieces.
4   *With flaying ... a feast* I demand your attendance at a feast of (or by means of) flaying
     strikes.
5   *These lurdans were slew* If only these worthless persons were slain.

KNIGHT 1.   My sovereign lord, dismay you right not!
They are but fools, their eloquence wanting,°   *deficient*
For in sorrow and care soon they shall be caught.   195
Against us they can make no disstanding.°   *resistance*

KNIGHT 2.   My lord, all such shall be brought before your
    audience°   *hearing*
And liven° under your domination,   *live*
Or else dammed to death with mortal sentence,
If we them get under our governation!°   *control*   200

HEROD.   Now this is to me a gracious exhortation,
And greatly rejoiceth to my spirits indeed!
Though these sots° against me make replication,°   *fools / resistence*
I will suffer none to spring of that kindred;
Some voice[1] in my land shall spread,   205
Privily or pertly,[2] in my land about.
While I have such men, I need not to dread°   *fear*
But that he shall be brought under, withouten doubt.

(*Here cometh the Emperor's messenger, thus saying to Herod.*[3])

MESSENGER.   Hail, prince of bounteousness!
Hail, mighty lord of to magnify![4]   210
Hail, most of worship° of to express!   *honor*
Hail, righteous ruler in thy regency!
My sovereign Tiberius, chief of chivalry,
His sovereign sond° hath sent to you here: *message*
He desireth you and prayeth on° each party°   *in / part*   215
To fulfill his commandment and desire.

(*Here he shall take the letters unto the king.*)

HEROD.   Be he secure I will not spare°   *neglect*
For to complish° his commandment: *accomplish*
With sharp swords to pierce them bare°   *defenseless*

---

1   *voice*   The MS has "woys"; the meaning of this line is somewhat obscure.
2   *Privily or pertly*   Secretly or openly.
3   *Here cometh ... Herod*   The word "messenger" does not appear in the manuscript but is
    supplied from context.
4   *of to magnify*   Worthy to praise.

220 In all countries within this regent,° *kingdom*
For his love to fulfill his intent.
None such shall from our hands start,° *escape*
For we will fulfill his royal judgment
With sword and spear to pierce them through the heart.[1]

225 But, Messenger, receive this letter with,° *forthwith*
And bear it unto Pilate's sight.
MESSENGER. My lord, it shall be done full wight;° *quickly*
In haste I will me speed.

PILATE.[2] Now royally I reign in robes of richesse,
230 Kid° and known both nigh° and far *acknowledged / near*
For judge of Jerusalem, the truth to express,
Under the Emperor, Tiberius Caesar.
Therefore I rede° you all: beware *advise*
Ye do no prejudice against the law!
235 For and° ye do, I will you not spare *if*
Till ye have judgment to be hanged and draw![3]

For I am Pilate, promissory° and president; *representative*
All renegade robbers improperate,°[4] *worthy of reproach*
To put them to pain, I spare for no pity.
240 My sergeants seemly, what say ye?
Of this rehearsed, I will not spare.
Pleasantly, sirs, answer to me,
For in my heart I shall have the less care.

SERGEANT 1. As ye have said, I hold it for the best,
245 If any such among us may we know.
SERGEANT 2. For to give them judgment I hold it best,
And so shall ye be dread° of high and low. *feared*

---

1 *Be he secure ... the heart* Several words in this stanza ("to" at 218, "them" at 219 and 224) are corrected following Baker et al.; the manuscript appears to be faulty here.

2 *PILATE* Pontius Pilate, the Roman governor of Judea, who ordered the execution of Jesus.

3 *hanged and draw* Hanged by the neck, after being dragged (drawn) to the gallows. This was a standard punishment for high treason in medieval England.

4 *improperate* The form in the text, "inperrowpent," is obscure. Baker, Murphy, and Hall (200 n.238) suggest this form as a possibility.

PILATE.   Ah, now I am restored to felicity.°   *happiness*

(*Here cometh the Emperor's messenger to Pilate.*)

MESSENGER.   Hail, royal in realm, in robes of richesse!
   Hail, present thou, prince's peer!   250
   Hail, judge of Jerusalem, the truth to express!
   Tiberius the Emperor sendeth writing here,
   And prayeth you, as you be his lover dear,
   Of this writing to take advisement
   In strengthening of his laws clear,   255
   As he hath set you in the state of judgment.

(*Here Pilate taketh the letters with great reverence.*)

PILATE.   Now, by Mars so mighty, I shall set many a snare
   His laws to strength° in all that I may.   *strengthen*
   I rejoice of his renown and of his welfare,
   And for thy tidings I give thee this gold today.   260
MESSENGER.   Ah, largess! Yea, lord, I cry this day,
   For· this is a gift of great degree!
PILATE.   Messenger, unto my sovereign thou say,
   On° the most special wise° recommend me!   *in / way*

(*Here avoideth° the messenger, and Cyrus taketh his death.*)   *exits*

CYRUS.   Ah, help, help! I stand in dread;   265
   Sickness is set under my side.
   Ah, help! Death will acquit° me my mede.°   *pay / reward*
   Ah, great God, thou be my guide!
   How I am troubled, both back and side;
   Now, withly,° help me to my bed.   *quickly* 270
   Ah! This rendeth my ribs! I shall never go° nor ride.   *walk*
   The dint° of death is heavier than lead.   *blow*
   Ah, Lord, Lord, what shall I do this tide?°   *time*
   Ah, gracious God, have ruth° on me,   *pity*
   In this world no longer to abide!   275
   I bless you, my children; God mote with us be!¹

(*Here avoideth° Cyrus suddenly, and then saying Lazarus:*)   *exits*

---

1   *God mote with us be*   May God be with us.

LAZARUS.   Alas, I am set in great heaviness.
There is no tongue my sorrow may tell,
So sore I am brought in distress.
280   In faintness I falter for° this fray° fell;°   *because of / conflict / dire*
This duress will let me no longer dwell°   *live*
But° God, of grace, soon me redress.   *unless*
Ah, how my pains don° me repel!°   *do / attack*
Lord, withstand this duress!

285   MARY MAGDALENE.   The *invictissimus*[1] God that ever shall reign,
Be his help, and soul's succor!
To whom it is most needful to complain,
He to bring us out of our dolor;°   *pain*
He is most mightiest governor,
290   From sorrowing us to restrain.°   *prevent*

MARTHA.   Ah, how I am set in sorrows sad,
That long my life I may not endure!
These grievous pains make me near mad!
Under clour° is now my father's cure,°   *heavy blow / care*
295   That sometime° was here, full merry and glad.   *formerly*
Our Lord's mercy be his measure,
And defend him from pains sad.°   *serious*

LAZARUS.   Now, sisters, our father's will we will express;
This castle is ours, with all the fee.°   *wealth*
300   MARTHA.   As head and governor, as reason is,
And on° this wise° abiden° with you will we.   *in / way / stay*
We will not dissever,° whatso°   *part company / whatever*
befall.°   *happens*
MARY MAGDALENE.   Now, brother and sister, welcome ye be,
And thereof specially° I pray you all.   *especially*

(*Here shall enter the King of the World, the Flesh, and the Devil,*[2]
with the Seven Deadly Sins,[3] *a Bad Angel, and a Good Angel, thus*
saying the World:)

---

1   *invictissimus*   Latin: mightiest.
2   *King of the World ... Devil*   The World, the Flesh, and the Devil: the three sources of
temptation to the soul. Here, they are represented as feudal lords, commanding armies of
evil spirits and vices.
3   *Seven Deadly Sins*   Pride, Envy, Wrath, Greed, Lechery, Gluttony, and Sloth.

WORLD. I am the World, worthiest that ever God wrought,° *made* 305
And also I am the primate portraiture
Next Heaven,[1] if the truth be sought,
And that I judge me to° Scripture.   *by reference to*
And I am he that longest shall endure,
And also most of domination.   310
If I be his foe, who is able to recure?°   *prosper*
For the Wheel of Fortune[2] with me hath set his center.

In me resteth the order of the metals seven,
The which to the seven planets are knit full sure:[3]
Gold pertaining to the Sun, as astronomers neven;°   *say* 315
Silver to the Moon white and pure;
Iron unto the Mars that long may endure;
The fugitive mercury unto Mercurius;
Copper unto Venus, red in his mirror;
The frangible° tin to Jupiter, if ye can discuss;   *fragile* 320

On this planet, Saturn full of rancor,°   *hostility*
This soft metal, lead, not of so great pureness.
Lo, all this rich treasure with the World doth endure,
The seven princes of Hell, of great bounteousness.
Now, who may presume to come to my honor?   325
PRIDE. Yea, worthy World, ye be grander of gladness

To them that dwell under your domination!
COVETISE. And whoso will not, he is soon set aside
Whereas° I, Covetise,° take   *wherever / greed*
ministration.°   *authority*
WORLD. Of that, I pray you, make no declaration!   330

---

1   *primate portraiture / Next Heaven* Closest representation of Heaven.
2   *Wheel of Fortune* An image from Boethius's *Consolation of Philosophy* (fifth century),
    one of the most popular and influential works in the medieval and early modern periods.
    All people live metaphorically on the rim of the wheel, so that their fortunes are always
    changing. The World here claims to live at the center of the wheel, and thus to be un-
    changing and eternal, like God.
3   *the metals seven ... full sure* This association of seven metals with the seven planets of
    the geocentric universe is common in medieval literature, as seen also, for example, in
    Chaucer's writings. The planets, named after pagan gods, were sometimes also associated
    with demonic powers and therefore with the Seven Deadly Sins.

Make such to know my sovereignty,
And then they shall be fain° to make supplication,   *glad*
If that they stand in any necessity.

(*Here shall enter the King of Flesh, with Sloth, Gluttony, Lechery.*)

FLESH.   I, King of Flesh, flourished° in my flowers,   *overflowing*
335   Of dainties° delicious I have great domination.   *delicacies*
　　　So royal a king was never borne in° bowers,°   ·   *into / bedrooms*
　　　Nor hath more delight, ne more delectation.
　　　For I have comfortatives to my comfortation:[1]
　　　Dia-galonga, ambra, and also margaretton.[2]
340   All this is at my list,° against all vexation.   *pleasure*

　　　All wicked things I will set aside.
　　　Clary, pepper long, with *granorum paradisi*,[3]
　　　Ginger and cinnamon at every tide:°   *time*
　　　Lo, all such dainty° delicacies use I.   *pleasing*

345   With such dainties I have my bliss.
　　　Who will covet° more game° and glee,°   *want / amusement / delight*
　　　My fair spouse Lechery to halse° and kiss?   *embrace*
　　　Here is my knight Gluttony, as good reason is,
　　　With this pleasant lady to rest by my side.
350   Here is Sloth, another goodly of to express;
　　　A more pleasant company doth nowhere abide.

LECHERY.   O ye prince, how I am full of ardent love,
　　　With sparkles° full of amorousness.   *sparks*
　　　With you to rest fain° would I approve,   *gladly*
355   To show pleasance to your gentleness.

---

1   *For I ... my comfortation*   For I have comforting substances for the purpose of comfort-
　　ing me. The King of Flesh proceeds to list the medicinal substances kept in his consider-
　　able personal infirmary.
2   *Dia-galonga ... margaretton*   Compound of galingale, ambergris, and also powdered
　　pearls. Such rare and expensive items would have functioned as medicinal ingredients.
　　Galingale is a rhizome of certain Asian plants related to ginger; ambergris is a waxy
　　substance found in the intestines of sperm whales.
3   *Clary*   Herb native to southern Europe; *pepper long*   Vine native to India; *grano-
　　rum paradisi*   Latin: grains of paradise. It is an African spice similar to peppercorns. All
　　of these materials would have been rare and expensive in medieval England.

FLESH.   O ye beauteous bird, I must you kiss;
I am full of lust to halse you this tide.

(*Here shall enter the Prince of Devils in a stage, and Hell
underneath that stage, thus saying the Devil.*)

SATAN.   Now I, prince peerless, pricked° in pride,   *dressed*
Satan, your sovereign, set with every circumstance,°   *advantage*
For I am attired° in my tower to tempt you this tide.   *equipped* 360
As a king royal I sit at my pleasance,
With Wrath and Envy at my royal retainance.°   *service*
The boldest in bower I bring to obey,
Man's soul to besiegen° and bring to   *besiege*
   obeisance.°   *submission*
Yea, with tide and time I do that I may,   365
For at him I have despite: that he should have the joy
That Lucifer, with many a legion, lost for their pride.
The snares that I shall set were never set at Troy;
So I think to besiegen him by every way wide.
I shall get him from grace wheresoever he abide;   370
That body and soul shall come to my hold,°   *stronghold*
Him for to take!
Now, my knights so stout,°   *steadfast*
With me ye shall run in rout,°   *troop*
My counsel to take, for a scout.[1]   375
Withly° that we were went° for my sake.   *quickly / gone*
WRATH.   With wrath or wiles we shall her win—
ENVY.   Or with some subtlety set her in sin.
SATAN.   Come off, then, let us begin
To work her some wrack.°   *misfortune* 380

(*Here shall the Devil go to the World with his company.*)

SATAN.   Hail, World, worthiest of abundance!
In haste we must a council take;
Ye must apply you with all your affiance°   *confidence*
A woman of worship our servant to make.

---

1   *With me ... for a scout*   The meaning is not entirely clear; one possible paraphrase is "You
shall assemble in formation with me on a surveillance mission, so that I may improve my
information."

385 WORLD.　Satan, with my counsel I will thee advance;
　　　I pray thee, come up unto my tent.
　　　Were the King of Flesh here with his assemblence°—　　*assembly*
　　　Messenger! Anon, that thou were went
　　　This tide!
390　　Say the King of Flesh with great renown,
　　　With his counsel that to him be boun,°　　　*bound*
　　　In all the haste that ever they maun,°　　　*may*
　　　Come as fast as he may ride.

　　SENSUALITY.　My lord, I am your servant Sensuality;
395　　Your message to don,° I am of glad cheer.　　*take*
　　　Right soon in presence ye shall him see,
　　　Your will for to fulfill here.

　　(*Here he goeth to the Flesh, thus saying:*)

　　　Hail, lord in land, led with liking!°　　　*pleasure*
　　　Hail, Flesh in lust,° fairest to behold!　　　*delight*
400　　Hail, lord and leader of emperor and king!
　　　The worthy World, by way° and wold,°　　　*road / forest*
　　　Hath sent for you and your council.
　　　Satan is sembled° with his household　　　*assembled*
　　　Your counsel to have, most for avail.

405 FLESH.　Hence in haste, that we there were;
　　　Let us make no longer delay.
　　SENSUALITY.　Great mirth to their hearts should you
　　　　you a-rear,°　　　*raise up*
　　　By my troth,[1] I dare safely say.

　　(*Here cometh the King of Flesh to the World, thus saying.*)

　　　FLESH.　Hail be you, sovereigns lief° and dear!　　*beloved*
410　　Why so hastily do ye for me send?
　　　WORLD.　Ah, we are right° glad we have you here,　*very*
　　　Our counsel together to comprehend.°　　　*include*
　　　Now, Satan, say your device.°　　　*scheme*
　　　SATAN.　Sirs, now ye be set,° I shall you say:　*seated*
415　Cyrus died this other day;

1　*By my troth*　By my pledge, i.e., I swear.

Now Mary, his daughter, that may,°   *maiden*
Of that castle beareth the price.¹

WORLD.   Certainly, sirs, I you tell,
   If she in virtue still° may dwell°   *always / remain*
   She shall be able to destroy Hell,   420
   But if² your counsel may otherwise devise.

FLESH.   Now ye, Lady Lechery, you must do your attendance,³
   For you be flower fairest of femininity.
   You shall go desire service and been at her attendance,⁴
   For ye shall soonest enter, ye beryl of beauty.   425

LECHERY.   Sirs, I obey your counsel in each degree;°   *step*
   Straightway thither° will I pass.°   *there / go*
SATAN.   *Spiritus maligni*⁵ shall come to thee,
   Her to tempt in every place.
   Now all the six that here be,   430

   Wisely to work, her favor to win,
   To enter her person by the labor of Lechery,
   That she at the last may come to Hell.

   How, how, *spiritus malignus*: thou wotest° what I mean   *know*
   Come out, I say! Hearest not what I say?   435

BAD ANGEL.   Sirs, I obey your counsel in each degree;
   Straightway thither will I pass.
   Speak soft, speak soft! I trot, her to tene;⁶
   I pray° thee pertly,° make no more noise.⁷   *ask / explicitly*

---

1   *beareth the price*   Holds the ownership.
2   *But if*   Unless.
3   *do your attendance*   Do your duty.
4   *been at her attendance*   Be at her service.
5   *Spiritus maligni*   Latin: Evil spirits.
6   *I trot, her to tene*   I hurry, in order to harm her.
7   *make no more noise*   The Bad Angel's admonitions for quiet may be directed towards the
   audience.

(Here shall all the Seven Deadly Sins besiege the castle till Mary agree to go to Jerusalem. Lechery shall enter the castle with the Bad Angel, thus saying Lechery:)

440 LECHERY.   Hail, lady most laudable° of alliance!   *praiseworthy*
          Hail, orient° as the sun in his reflexity!°   *dawnlike / brightness*
          Much° people be comforted by your benign   *many*
             affiance;°   *trust*
          Brighter than the burnished is your beams of beauty,
          Most debonarius[1] with your angelic delicity!°   *delightfulness*
445 MARY MAGDALENE.   What person be ye, that thus me commend?
     LECHERY.   Your servant to be, I would comprehend. °   *accomplish*

     MARY MAGDALENE.   Your debonarius obedience ravisheth me to
          tranquility.
          Now, since ye desire in each degree,
          To receive you I have great delectation.°   *delight*
450   Ye be heartily welcome unto me;
          Your tongue is so amiable, divided° with reason.   *marked out*

     LECHERY.   Now, good lady, will ye me express
          Why may there no gladness to you resort?°   *come*
     MARY MAGDALENE.   For my father I have had great heaviness;
455   When I remember, my mind waxeth° mort.°   *becomes / dead*
     LECHERY.   Yea, lady, for all that, be of good comfort,
          For such abusions° may breed much disease.°   *injuries / discomfort*
          Such deceptions putteth pains to export;[2]
          Print° you in sports° which best doth you   *focus / entertainments*
             please!

460 MARY MAGDALENE.   Forsooth,° ye be welcome to mine   *truly*
          audience;°   *hearing*
          Ye be my heart's leech.°   *healer*
          Brother Lazarus, and° it be your pleasance,°   *if / pleasure*
          And ye, sister Martha, also, in substance
          This place I commend° unto your governance,   *commit*

---

1   *debonarius* Debonair. The English word "debonair" derives from French *de bon air*, having a good air; here it is incorrectly Latinized.
2   *Such ... export* Make an effort to put aside such disappointments.

And unto God I you beteach.°   ·   *recommend*   465

LAZARUS.   Now, sister, we shall do your intent,
In this place to be resident
While that ye be absent,
To keep this place from wretch.°   *harm*

(*Here taketh Mary her way to Jerusalem with Lechery, and they
shall resort to a taverner. Thus saying the taverner:*)

TAVERNER.   I am a taverner, witty° and wise,   *clever*   470
That wines have to sell, great plenty;
Of all the taverners, I bear the prize[1]
That be dwelling within the city.
Of wines I have great plenty,

Both white wine and red that is[2] so clear.   475

Here is wine of Malta, and malmseyn;°   *malmsey (a fortified wine)*
Clary wine, and claret, and other mo;°   *more*
Wine of Guelders and of Gaul; that made at the Groine,
Wine of Guyenne and Vernage,[3] I say also;
There be no better as far as ye can go!   480

LECHERY.   Lo, lady, the comfort and the succor:
Go we near and take a taste;
This shall bring your sprits to favor.
Taverner, bring us of the finest thou hast!
TAVERNER.   Here, lady, is wine, a repast,°   *refreshment*   485
To man and woman a good restorative.
Ye shall not think your money spent in waste;
From studies° and heaviness° it will you relieve.   *anxiety / sadness*

MARY MAGDALENE.   Iwis,° ye say sooth,° ye   *indeed / truth*
   groom° of bliss.   *servant*
To me ye be courteous and kind.   490

(*Here shall enter a gallant,° thus saying:*)   *lover*

---

1   *I bear the prize*   I am the best.
2   *is*   The word "is" is not in the manuscript.
3   *Wine of Guelders ... Vernage*   The taverner's wines come from various places in western
    Europe. His trade circles are small compared to those of Flesh.

PRIDE.[1] Huff, huff, huff! A fresh new gallant!
 Ware° of thirst, lay that adown!   *beware*
 What? Ween° ye, sirs, that I were a merchant,   *believe*
 Because that I am new come to town?
495 With some pretty tapster would I fain round.[2]
 I have a shirt of Raines,° with sleeves pendant,° *fine linen / flowing*
 A lace of silk for my lady constant.
 Ah, how she is beautiful and resplendent!

 When I am from her presence, Lord, how I sigh!
500 I will a-vie° sovereigns, and subjects I disdain.   *strive with*
 In winter a stomacher,[3] in summer, none at all;
 My doublet[4] and my hoses° ever together abide.   *stockings*
 I will, ere° even,° be shaven for to seem young. *before / evening*
 With hair against the hair, I love much playing;
505 That maketh me elegant and lusty° in liking.° *delightful / pleasure*
 Thus I live in this world, I do it for no pride.

LECHERY. Lady, this man is for you, as I see can,
 To set you in sports and talking this tide.°   *time*
MARY MAGDALENE. Call him in, taverner, as ye my love will
  have,
510 And we shall make full merry if he will abide.
TAVERNER. How, how, my master Curiosity!
PRIDE. What is your will, sir? What will ye with me?
TAVERNER. Here are gentlewomen, desire your presence to see,
 And for to drink with you this tide.

515 PRIDE. Ah, dear duchess, my daisy's eye,
 Splendent° of color, most of femininity,   *shining*
 Your sovereign colors set with sincerity,
 Consider my love unto your ally,

---

1 *PRIDE* In the MS this character is called both Gallant and Curiosity in the speech attributions to this scene; at 550, however, he is revealed to be Pride in disguise. As such, in this edition he is labeled Pride throughout.

2 *With some ... fain round* I would happily speak privately with some pretty barmaid.

3 *stomacher* Undergarment worn over the chest and stomach.

4 *doublet* Close-fitting men's jacket, fashionable in the late medieval and early modern periods.

Or else I am smote° with pains of perplexity.   *struck*

MARY MAGDALENE. Why, sir, ween° ye that I were a   *believe* 520
kell?[1]
PRIDE. Nay, princess, pardi,° ye be my heart's heal,   *indeed*
So would to God ye would my love feel.

MARY MAGDALENE. What cause that ye love me so suddenly?
PRIDE. O, needs I must, mine own lady.
Your person, it is so womanly   525
I cannot refrain me, sweet lily.

MARY MAGDALENE. Sir, courtesy doth it you lere.°   *teach*
PRIDE. Now, gracious ghost° withouten peer,   *spirit*
Much nurture° is that ye con.°   *refinement / know*
But will you dance, my own dear?   530
MARY MAGDALENE. Sir, I assent in good manner.
Go ye before, I sue° you near,   *follow*
For a man at all times beareth reverence.

PRIDE. Now, by my troth, ye be with other teen.°   *distress*
Fall° apace,° taverner, let us seen:°   *come / quickly / see* 535
Sops in wine, how love ye those?[2]
MARY MAGDALENE. As ye do, so doth me.
I am right glad that met be we;
My love in you ginneth° to close!°   *begins / be confirmed*

PRIDE. Now, darling dear, will you do by my rede?°   *advice* 540
We have drunken, and ate little bread;
Will we walk to another stead?°   *place*
MARY MAGDALENE. Even at your will, my dear darling.
Though ye will go to the world's end,
I will never from you wend,°   *go* 545
To die for your sake.

---

1   *kell* Woman's headdress. The term's exact sense here is not entirely certain, but it seems
    from the context to refer either to sexual licentiousness, lowliness of class, or both.
2   *those* The MS does not include "those"; most modern editors add the word for the sake
    of the meter and rhyme scheme.

(Here shall Mary and the gallant avoid,° and the Bad Angel   exit
goeth to the World, the Flesh, and the Devil, thus saying the Bad
Angel:)

BAD ANGEL.   Ah, lords! Ah, lords! Lords all at once!
    Ye have a servant fair and affable,°   *willing, courteous*
    For she is fallen in our grudgely grooms.[1]
550   Yea, Pride, called Curiosity, to her is full laudable,°   *praiseworthy*
    And to her he is most praisable,
    For she hath granted him all his boons.°   *wishes*
    She thinketh his person so amiable
    To her sight, he is seemlier than any king in thrones.

555 SATAN.   Ah, how I tremble and trot for these tidings!
    She is a sovereign servant that hath her fetched in sin.[2]
    Go thou again, and ever° be her guide.   *forever*
    The laudable life of lechery let her never lin,°   *leave*
    For of her all Hell shall make rejoicing.

(Here goeth the Bad Angel to Mary again.)

560 SATAN.   Farewell, farewell, ye two noble kings this tide,
    For home in haste I will me dress.°   *direct*
WORLD.   Farewell, Satan, Prince of Pride!
FLESH.   Farewell, seemliest, all sorrows to cease!

(Here shall Satan go home to his stage, and Mary shall enter into
the place[3] alone save the Bad Angel. And all the Seven Deadly Sins
shall be conveyed into the house of Simon Leprous; they shall be
arrayed like seven devils, thus kept close.[4] Mary shall be in an arbor,
thus saying:)

---

1 *For she ... grudgely grooms*   For she has fallen in with our malevolent servants.
2 *hath her fetched in sin*   Has brought herself into sin.
3 *enter into the place*   Enter into the playing-space. Like many plays of its period, this play
  seems to take place both on a set of elevated stages, representing specific and fixed locations, and on a flat area in between them, representing various undefined and transitional
  locations.
4 *thus kept close*   In this way kept hidden. The expulsion of the Seven Deadly Sins at 691
  is meant to be surprising and spectacular.

MARY MAGDALENE.   Ah, God be with my valentines,
My birds sweeting, my loves so dear,   565
For they be bought for a blossom of bliss.
Me marvelleth sore[1] they be not here.
But I will rest in this arbor°   *shaded garden*
Amongst these balms° precious of price,   *scented trees*
Till some lover will appear   570
That me is wont° to halse° and kiss.   *accustomed / embrace*

(*Here shall Mary lie down and sleep in the arbor.*)

SIMON LEPROUS.   This day wholly I put in remembrance
To solace° my guests to° my power;   *comfort / according to*
I have ordained° a dinner of substance,   *arranged*
My chief friends therewith to cheer.°   *entertain* 575
Into the seat I will appear
For my guests to make purveyance,°   *preparation*
For time draweth nigh to go to dinner,
And my officers be ready with their ordinance.°   *arrangements*

So would to God I might have acquaintance   580
Of the Prophet of true perfectness
To come to my place and purveyance;
It would rejoice my heart in great gladness.
For the report of his high nobleness
Runneth in countries far and near: 585
His preaching is of great perfectness,
Of rightwiseness° and mercy clear.   *righteousness*

(*Here enter Simon into the place. The Good Angel thus saying to Mary:*)

GOOD ANGEL.   Woman, woman, why art thou so
   unstable?°   *disobedient*
Full bitterly this bliss, it will be bought.
Why art thou against God so variable?°   *fickle* 590
Why, thinkest thou not God made thee of naught?
In sin and sorrow thou art brought;

---

1   *Me marvelleth sore*   It amazes me greatly.

Fleshly lust is to thee full delectable.
Salve° for thy soul must be sought,   *medicine*
595 And leave thy works vain and variable.

Remember, woman, for thy poor pride,
How thy soul shall liven° in Hell-fire.   *live*
Ah, remember how sorrowful it is to abide
Withouten end in anger and ire.
600 Remember thee on mercy; make thy soul clear.
I am the ghost° of goodness that so would thee guide.   *spirit*

MARY MAGDALENE.   Ah, how the spirit of goodness
        hath prompted me this tide,
And tempted me with title of true perfectness.
Alas, how bitterness in my heart doth abide!
605 I am wounded with works of great distress.
Ah, how pensiveness putteth me to oppress,[1]
That I have sinned on every side!
O Lord, who shall put me from this painfulness?
Ah, who shall to mercy be my ghostly guide?

610 I shall pursue the Prophet, whereso he be,
For he is the well of perfect charity.
By the oil of mercy, he shall me relieve
With sweet balms. I will seek him this sith,°   *time*
And sadly° follow his lordship in each degree.   *seriously*

(*Here shall enter the Prophet with his disciples. Thus saying Simon
Leprous:*)

615 SIMON LEPROUS.   Now ye be welcome, master, most of
        magnificence!
I beseech° you benignly, ye will be so gracious,   *beg*
If that it be liking° unto your high presence,   *pleasing*
This day to come dine at my house.

JESUS.   God-a-mercy,° Simon, that thou   *God have mercy*
        wilt° me know.   *wish to*
620 I will enter thy house with peace and unity.°   *harmony*

---

1   *Ah, how ... to oppress* Ah, how reflection makes me overwhelmed.

I am glad for to rest there° grace ginneth°   *where / begins to*
    grow,
For within thy house shall rest charity,
And the beams of grace shall be illuminous.
But since thou vouchsafe° a dinner on° me,   *give / to*
With peace and grace I enter thy house.   625

SIMON LEPROUS.   I thank you, master most benign and gracious,
That you will of your high sovereignty.
To me it is a joy most spacious,°   *large*
Within my house that I may you see.

Now sit to the board,° masters all!   *table*   630

(*Here shall Mary follow along, with this lamentation.*)

MARY MAGDALENE.   Oh, I, cursed caitiff,° that much   *wretch*
    woe hath wrought°   *made*
Against my maker of mights most!
I have offended him with deed and thought;
But in his grace is all my trust
Or else I know well I am but lost,   635

Body and soul damned perpetual!
Yet, good Lord of Lords, my hope perennial
With thee to stand in grace and favor to see:
Thou knowest my heart and thought in especial;
Therefore, good Lord, after my heart reward me!   640

(*Here shall Mary wash the feet of the Prophet with the tears of
her eyes, wiping them with her hair, and then anoint him with a
precious ointment. Jesus dicit:*[1])

JESUS.   Simon, I thank thee specially
For this great repast° that here hath be.   *meal*
But Simon, I tell thee factually,
I have things to say to thee.
SIMON LEPROUS.   Master, what your will be,   645
And° it please you, I will you hear;   *if*

---

1   *dicit*   Latin: says.

Sayeth your liking[1] unto me,
And all the pleasance of your mind and desire.

JESUS.   Simon, there was a man in this present life,
650   The which° had two debtors well sure,°   *who / indeed*
      The which were poor, and might make no restorative,°   *repayment*
      But still in their debt did endure.°   *remain*
      The one owed him an hundred pence full sure,
      And the other fifty, so befell° the chance.   *happened*
655   And because he could not his money recure,°   *recover*
      They asked him forgiveness, and he forgave in substance.[2]

      But, Simon, I pray thee, answer me to this sentence:
      Which of these two persons was most beholden° to   *indebted*
        that man?
      SIMON LEPROUS.   Master, and° it please your high   *if*
        presence,
660   He that most owed him, as my reason give can.
      JESUS.   *Recte judicasti.*[3] Thou art a wise man,
      And this question hast deemed° truly.   *judged*
      If thou in thy conscience remember can,
      Ye two[4] be the debtors that I of specify.

665   But Simon, behold this woman in all wise:°   *ways*
      How she, with tears of her bitter weeping,
      She washeth my feet and doth me service;
      And anointeth them with ointments, lowly kneeling;
      And with her hair, fair and bright-shining,
670   She wipeth them again with good intent.

      But Simon, since that I entered thy house,
      To wash my feet thou didst not apply,
      Nor to wipe my feet thou were not so favorous.°   *generous*

---

1   *Sayeth your liking*   Say what you please.
2   *They asked ... in substance*   They asked him to cancel their loans, and he canceled their
    loans in full.
3   *Recte judicasti*   Latin: Thou hast judged rightly (Luke 7.43).
4   *Ye two*   I.e., Simon Leprous and Mary Magdalene.

Wherefore, in thy conscience, thou oughtst not to reply.
But woman, I say to thee verily,°   *truly*   675
I forgive thee thy wretchedness;
And whole in soul be thou made thereby.

MARY MAGDALENE.   O blessed be thou, Lord of everlasting life,
And blessed be thy birth of that pure virgin!
Blessed be thou, repast contemplative,[1]   680
Against my sickness health and medicine!

And for that° I have sinned in the sin of pride,   *because*
I will inhabit° me with humility.   *clothe*
Against wrath and envy, I will divide°   *distribute*
These fair virtues: patience and charity.   685

JESUS.   Woman, in contrition thou art expert,
And in thy soul hast inward might
That sometime were in desert,
And from darkness hast purchased light.[2]
Thy faith hath saved thee and made thee bright,   690
Wherefore I say to thee, *vade in pace.*[3]

(*With this word seven devils shall devoid° from*   *depart*
the woman, and the Bad Angel enter into Hell with thunder.)

MARY MAGDALENE.   O thou, glorious Lord, this
    rehearsed° for my speed,°   *declared / success*
Soul-health at this time for to recure.°   *restore*
Lord, for that° I was in wanhope,° now stand   *because / despair*
    I in dread°   *fear*
But that° thy great mercy with me may endure.   *unless*   695
My thought thou knewest withouten any doubt.
Now may I trust the teaching of Isaiah in Scripture,
Whose report of thy nobleness runneth far about.

---

1   *repast contemplative* Spiritual food.
2   *Woman, in ... purchased light* Woman, you are excellent in contrition, and you have
    inward strength in your soul, you who were once in the wilderness, and who has attained
    light from the darkness.
3   *vade in pace* Latin: go in peace.

JESUS.   Blessed be they at all time
700   That seen° me not and have me in credence.°   *see / belief*
        With contrition thou hast made a recompense
        Thy soul to save from all distress.
        Beware, and keep thee from all negligence,
        And after thou shalt be partner of my bliss.

        (*Here devoideth° Jesus with his disciples. The Good*   *exits*
        Angel rejoicing of Magdalene.)

705 GOOD ANGEL.   Holy God, highest of omnipotency,
        The estate of good governance to thee I recommend,
        Humbly beseeching thine imperial glory
        In thy divine virtue us to comprehend.°   *encompass*

        And delectable Jesus, sovereign sapience,°   *wisdom*
710   Our faith we recommend unto your pure pity,
        Most meekly praying to your holy appearance:
        Illumine° our ignorance with your divinity!   *enlighten*

        Ye be cleped° redemption of souls' defense,   *called*
        Which shall be obscured by thy blessed mortality.
715   O *lux vera*,[1] grant us your license,°   *permission*
        That with the spirit of error I not seduced be!

        And, *Spiritus Almae*,[2] to you most benign,
        Three persons in Trinity and one God etern,°   *eternal*
        Most lowly° our faith we consign°   *humbly / confirm*
720   That we may come to your bliss glorified from malign,°   *evil*
        And with your ghostly° bread to feed us,   *spiritual*
            we desiren.°   *desire*

    SATAN.   Ah! Out, out, and harrow![3] I am hampered with hate!
        In haste will I set our judgment to see;
        With these beetle-browed bitches I am at debate:
725   How, Belfagour and Beelzebub! Come up here to me!

---

1   *lux vera*   Latin: true light.
2   *Spiritus Almae*   Latin: Holy Spirit; literally, Spirit of the Soul.
3   *Out, out, and harrow!*   A cry used to call for help or to express distress.

(*Here appeareth two devils before the master.*)

DEVIL 2.   Here, lord, here! What will ye?[1]
SATAN.   The judgment of harlots here to see,
Sitting in judicial-like estate.

How, thou Bad Angel! Appear before my grace!
BAD ANGEL.   As flat as fox I fall before your face.   730
SATAN.   Thou thief! Why hast thou done all this trespass:
To let yon° woman thy bonds break?   *that*
BAD ANGEL.   The Spirit of Grace sore° did her smite,°   *hard / hit*
And tempted so sore that hypocrite!
SATAN.   Yea, these hard baleys° on thy buttocks shall   *rods*   735
   bite!
In haste! On thee I will be wreak!°   *avenged*

Come up, ye whoresons,[2] and score° away the itch,   *cut*
And with this pain ye do him pitch!°   *pay*
Come off,° ye harlots,° that it were done!   *quickly / villains*

(*Here shall they serve all the seven as they do the first.*[3])

SATAN.   Now have I a part of my desire.   740
Go into this house,[4] ye lurdans° here,   *villains*
And look ye set it on a fire;
And that shall them awake!

(*Here shall the other devils set the house on a fire, and make a soot,
and Mary shall go to Lazarus and to Martha.*)

SATAN.   So, now have we well affrayed° these felons   *attacked*
   false.

---

1   *DEVIL 2 … will ye?*   Oddly, the First Devil does not speak, and the following speech
    (clearly spoken by Satan and assigned by most editors thereto) is given to a third devil in
    the MS.
2   *whoresons*   Literally, sons of whores: a common insult in late medieval and early modern
    England.
3   *Here shall … the first*   That is, the Seven Deadly Sins and the Bad Angel are all whipped.
4   *Go into this house*   That is, the prison-house into which the Seven Deadly Sins and the
    Bad Angel have been placed.

745 They be blazed,° both body and halls.   *burned*
     Now to Hell let us sink als,°   *also*
     To our fellows black.

     MARY MAGDALENE.   O brother, my heart's consolation;
     O blessed in life and solitary!
750 The blessed Prophet, my comfortation,
     He hath made me clean and delectary,°   *delightful*
     The which was to sin a subjectary.
     This King, Christ, considered his creation;
     I was drenchen° in sin diversary°   *drowned / manifold*
755 Till that Lord relieved me by his domination.

     Grace to me he would never deny;
     Though I were never so sinful, he said *revertere*. [1]
     Oh, I, sinful creature, to grace I will apply;
     The oil of mercy hath healed mine infirmity.

760 MARTHA.   Now worshipped be that high name Jesu,
     The which in Latin is called Savior,
     Fulfilling that word even of due:°   *right*
     To all sinful and sick, he is succor.
     LAZARUS.   Sister, ye be welcome unto your tower.
765 Glad in heart of your obeisance,
     While that I live I will serve him with honor,
     That ye have forsaken sin and variance.°   *waywardness*

     MARY MAGDALENE.   Christ, that is the light and the clear day,
     He hath incurred° the darkness of the cloudy night;   *suffered*
770 Of light the lucence,° and light very,°   *brilliance / true*
     Whose preaching to us is a gracious light;
     Lord, we beseech thee, as thou art most of might,
     Out of the dead sleep of darkness defend us aye!°   *always*
     Give us grace ever to rest° in light,   *remain*
775 In quiet and in peace to serve thee, night and day.

     (*Here shall Lazarus take his death, thus saying:*)

     _____

     1 *revertere* Latin: turn again.

LAZARUS.   Ah, help! Help, sisters, for charity!
Alas! Death is set at my heart.
Ah, lay on hands; where are ye?
Ah, I falter and fall; I wax° all unquert;°   *become / distressed*
Ah, I boom above, I wax all swart,[1]   780
Ah, good Jesus, thou be my guide!
Ah, no longer now I revert;°   *recover*
I yield up the ghost; I may not abide.°   *stay*

MARY MAGDALENE.   O, good brother! Take comfort and might,
And let none° heaviness in your heart abide.   *no*   785
Let° away all this faintness and fright,   *leave*
And we shall get you leeches° your pains to   *healers*
    divide.°   *mitigate*

MARTHA.   Ah, I sigh and sorrow, and say alas;
This sorrow is appoint to be my confusion.
Gentle sister, hie° we from this place,   *go*   790
For the Prophet to him hath great delectation.°   *delight*
Good brother, take some comfortation,

For we will go to seek your cure.

(*Here goeth Mary and Martha, and meet with Jesus, thus saying:*)

MARY MAGDALENE AND MARTHA.   O Lord Jesus, our mellifluous
    sweetness,
Thou art greatest Lord in glory!   795
Lover to thee, Lord, in all lowliness,
Comfort thy creatures that to thee cry!
Behold your lover, good Lord, specially,
How Lazarus lieth sick in great distress.
He is thy lover, Lord, surely.   800
Unbind him, good Lord, of his heaviness!

JESUS.   Of all infirmity, there is none to° death;   *like*
For of all pains, that is impossible

---

1 *Ah, I ... all swart* Ah, there is a noise in my head; everything grows dark.

To understand by reason. To know the work,
805 The joy that is in Jerusalem Heavenly,
Can never be compiled° by cunning° of   *listed / cleverness*
    clerk:°   *scholar*
To see the joys of the Father in glory,
The joys of the Son which ought to be magnified,°   *praised*
And of the Third Person, the Holy Ghost, truly,
810 And all three but one, in Heaven glorified.

Now, women that arn° in my presence here,   *are*
Of my words take advisement.
Go home again to your brother Lazar;
My grace to him shall be sent.

815 MARY MAGDALENE.   O, thou glorious Lord here present,
We yield to thy salutation.
In our ways we be expedient.
Now, Lord, us defend from tribulation!

(*Here goeth Mary and Martha homeward, and Jesus
devoideth.*)

LAZARUS.   Ah! In woe I welter,° as waves in the wind.   *thrash*
820 Away is went° all my succor.   *gone*
Ah, Death, Death, thou art unkind.°   *monstrous*
Ah! Ah, now bursteth mine heart! This is a sharp shower.
Farewell, my sisters, my bodily health.

(*Mortuus est.*[1])

MARY MAGDALENE.   Jesus, my Lord, be your succor,
825 And he must be your ghost's° wealth!   *spirit's*

KNIGHT 1.   God's grace mote° be his governor,   *must*
In joy everlasting for to be.
KNIGHT 2.   Among all good souls send him favor,
As thy power is most of dignity.

---

1 *Mortuus est* Latin: He is dead.

MARTHA.   Now, since the chance is fallen so,   830
   That death hath drawn him down this day,
   We must needs our devoirs° do   *duties*
   To the earth to bring him, without delay.
MARY MAGDALENE.   As the use° is now, and hath   *custom*
      been aye,°   *always*
   With weepers to the earth you him bring.   835
   All this must be done as I you say,
   Clad in black, withouten lessing.°   ·   *diminishment*

KNIGHT 3.   Gracious ladies of great honor,
   This people is come here in your sight,
   Weeping and wailing with great dolor°   *agony*   840
   Because of my lord's death.

(*Here the one knight makes ready the stone, and the other brings in
the weepers arrayed in black.*)

KNIGHT 3.   Now, good friends that here be,
   Take up this body with good will
   And lay it in his sepulcher, seemly to see.
   Good Lord, him save from all manner ill!   845

(*Lay him in. Here all the people resort to the castle, thus saying
Jesus:*)

JESUS.   Time is come of very° cognition.°   *true / understanding*
   My disciples, go with me
   For to fulfill possible petition.[1]
   Go we together into Judea;
   There Lazar, my friend, is he.   850
   Go we together as children of light,
   And, from grievous sleep, save him will we!

DISCIPLES.   Lord, it please your mighty volunty,°   *will*
   Though he sleep, he may be saved by skill.

---

1   *For to ... petition*   In order to grant a request that lies within our power.

855 JESUS.   That is true, and by possibility;
        Therefore, of my death show you I will.

        My Father, of nimious° charity,   *very great*
        Sent me, his Son, to make redemption,
        Which was conceived by pure virginity,
860   And so in my mother had clear° incarnation.   *sinless*
        And therefore must I suffer grievous passion°   *agony*
        Under Pontius Pilate, with great perplexity:
        Beaten, bobbed,° scorned, crowned with thorn;   *struck*
        All this shall be the sufferance of my deity.°   *divinity*

865   Aye,° therefore, hastily follow me now,   *yes*
        For Lazar is dead, verily° to prove.   *truly*
        Wherefore° I am joyful, I say unto you,   *therefore*
        That I knowledge° you therewith that ye may it   *teach*
            believe.

        (*Here shall Jesus come with his disciples, and one Jew telleth
        Martha:*)

        JEW.   Ah, Martha, Martha, be full of gladness,
870   For the Prophet is coming, I say truly,
        With his disciples, in great lowliness;°   *humility*
        He shall you comfort with his mercy.

        (*Here Martha shall run against° Jesus, thus saying:*)   *towards*

        MARTHA.   Ah, Lord, me, simple creature, not deny
        Though I be wrapped in wretchedness!
875   Lord, and° thou hadst been here, verily,°   *if / truly*
        My brother had not a-been dead; I know well this.

        JESUS.   Martha, daughter, unto thee I say
        Thy brother shall rise again.
        MARTHA.   Yea, Lord, at the last day,
880   That I believe full plain.

JESUS. I am the resurrection of life that ever shall reign,
And whoso believeth verily in me
Shall have life everlasting, the sooth° to sayn.°   *truth / say*
Martha, believest thou this?
MARTHA. Yea, forsooth,° the Prince of Bliss!   *indeed*   885
I believe in Christ the Son of Sapience,°   *wisdom*
Which without end reign shall he,
To redeemen° us frail° from our iniquity.   *redeem / weak ones*

(*Here Mary shall fall° to° Jesus, thus saying Mary:*)   *kneel / before*

MARY MAGDALENE. O, thou rightwise° regent,   *righteous*
reigning in equity,
Thou gracious Lord, thou sweet Jesus!   890
And° thou haddest° been here, my brother alive   *if / had*
had be.°   *been*
Good Lord, mine heart doth this discuss.°   *judge*

JESUS. Where have ye put him? Say° me this.   *tell*
MARY MAGDALENE. In his monument, Lord, is he.
JESUS. To that place ye me wis;°   *guide*   895
That grave I desire to see.

Take off the stone of this monument;

The agreement° of grace here show I will.   *joy*

MARTHA. Ah, Lord, your precept fulfilled shall be.
This stone I remove with glad cheer.   900
Gracious Lord, I ask thee mercy;
Thy will mote° be fulfilled here.   *may*

(*Here shall Martha put off the gravestone.*)

JESUS. Now Father, I beseech thine high paternity°   *fatherhood*
That my prayer be resoundable° to thy fatherhood   *proclaimed*
in glory,
To open thine ears to thy Son in humanity:°   *human form*   905
Not only for me, but for thy people verily,°   *truly*

That they may believe, and betake° to thy mercy.   *commit*
Father, for them I make supplication;
Gracious Father, grant me my boon.°   *wish*

910 Lazar, Lazar! Come hither° to me!   *here*

(*Here shall Lazarus arise, trussed° with   wrapped*
towels, in a sheet.)

LAZARUS.   Ah, my Maker, my Savior, blessed mote° thou be!   *may*
Here men may know thy works of wonder;
Lord, nothing is unpossible° to thee,   *impossible*
For my body and my soul was departed asunder.
915 I should 'a° rotted as doth the tinder,   *have*
Flesh from the bones a-consumed away.
Now is aloft° that late° was under;   *above (ground) / formerly*

The goodness of God hath done for me here,
For he is boot° of all bales° to unbind,°   *help / evils / free*
920 That blessed Lord that here did appear!

(*Here all the people, and the Jews, Mary, and Martha, with one*
voice, say these words: "We believe in you, Savior, Jesus, Jesus, Jesus!")

JESUS.   Of your good hearts I have advertations,°   *notice*
Wherethrough in soul, whole made ye be.
Betwixt you and me be never variations,°   *disagreement*
Wherefore I say *vade in pace.*[1]

(*Here devoideth Jesus with his disciples. Mary*
and Martha and Lazarus go home to the castle.
And here beginneth the King of Marseilles his boast.[2])

925 KING.   Avaunt!° Avaunt thee, unworthy wretches!   *get out*
Why lout° ye not low to my laudable°   *bow / praiseworthy*
   presence,

---

1   *vade in pace*   Latin: go in peace.
2   *Here devoideth ... his boast*   The phrase "the King of Marseilles" is added for clarity. Note
    the transcription of this page (folio 116r) in the appendix.

Ye brawling° breels,° and   *quarrelsome / wretches*
   blabber-lipped° bitches,   *mouthy*
Obediently to obey me without offense?

I am a sovereign seemly.° That ye see but seld:°   *fitting / seldom*
None such under sun, the sooth° for to say.   *truth*   930
When I fare° freshly and fierce to the field,°   *go / battlefield*
My foemen flee for fear of my fray!°   *attack*
Even as an emperor I am honored ay,

When banners gin° to blaze,° and beams°   *begin / display / horns*
   gin to blow.
Head am I, highest of all Heathenness°   *pagan lands*   935
   hold;°   *regarded*
Both kings and kaisers,° I will they shall me know,   *chiefs*
Or else they buy the bargain[1] that ever they were so bold!
I am King of Marseilles, tales to be told;
Thus I would it were known far and near!
Who say contrarily, I cast him in cares cold,   940
And he shall buy the bargain wonder°   *exceedingly*
   dear.°   *expensively*

I have a favorous° food,° and fresh as the   *pleasing / ward*
   falcon;
She is full° fair° in her femininity.   *completely / beautiful*
When I look on this lady, I am lusty as the lion
In my sight;   945
Of delicity° most delicious,   *delight*
Of fellowship most felicious,°   *joyous*
Of all foods most favorous:
O, my bliss, in beauties bright!

QUEEN.   O of conditions,[2] and most honorable,   950
   Lowly° I thank you for this recommendation,   *humbly*
   The bountiest,° and the boldest under banner   *most generous*
     bright,

---

1 *buy the bargain* Pay the price.
2 *O of conditions* O you of excellent qualities.

No creature so coruscant° to my consolation.　　　　　*glittering*
When the regent be resident, it is my refection.[1]
955　Your delectable deeds divideth° me from　　　　*keep away*
　　diversity.°　　　　　　　　　　　　　　　　　*conflict*
In my person I provide to put me from pollution;[2]
To be pleasant to your person, it is my prosperity.

　KING.　Now, God-a-mercy, beryl brightest of beauty!
　　God-a-mercy, ruby ruddy as the rose!
960　Ye be so pleasant to my pay,° ye put° me from　　*satisfaction / keep*
　　pain.
Now, comely° knights, look that ye forth dress°　　*pleasing / bring*
Both spices and wine here in haste!

*(Here shall the knights get spices and wine. And here shall enter a
devil in horrible array, thus saying:)*

　DEVIL.　Out, out, harrow! I may cry and yell,
　For lost is all our labor, wherefore I say alas!
965　For of all holds° that ever hurt, none so as Hell!　　*prisons*
Our bars of iron are all to-burst,° strong gates of　　*broken apart*
　　brass.
The King of Joy entered in thereat,[3] as bright as fire's blaze;
For fray° of his fearful banner our　　　　　　　*attack*
　　fellowship° fled asunder.°　　　　　　　*company / apart*
When he touched it, with his touching they burst as any glass,
970　And rove° asunder, as it been° with　　　*cracked / as if it had been*
　　thunder!

Now are we thrall° that first° were free,　　　*enslaved / previously*
By the Passion of his manhood.
On a cross on high hanged was he,
Which hath destroyed our labor and all our deed!

1　*When ... refection*　When the king is at home, it is my comfort.
2　*In my ... from pollution*　I take care to keep myself away from impurity.
3　*Our bars ... in thereat*　The Devil is describing the Harrowing of Hell, in which Jesus,
　　between his death on Good Friday and resurrection on Easter Sunday, breaks open the
　　gates of Hell and frees its virtuous prisoners, such as Abraham, Sarah, and Moses. This
　　episode, first described in the apocryphal (fifth century CE) Gospel of Nicodemus, was a
　　popular subject for medieval art and drama.

He hath lightened° Limbo,[1] and to Paradise yede;°   *emptied / gone*   975
That wonderful work worked us wrack.[2]
Adam, and Abraham, and all their kindred,
Out of our prison to joy were they take.°   *taken*

All this hath been wrought° since Friday at noon;[3]   *done*
Burst down our gates that hanged were full high!   980
Now is he risen—his resurrection is done—
And is proceeded into Galilee.
With many a temptation we touched him to atry,°   *test*
To know whether he was God or none.
Yet for all our business,° bleared is our eye,   *effort*   985
For with his wild work he hath won them,
   everichon!°   *every single one*
Now for the time to come,
Their shall none fall to our chance°   *fate*
But° at his deliverance,   *except*
And weighed by rightful balance,   990
And given by rightful doom.°   *judgement*
I tell you all, in sum, to Hell will I gone!°   *go*

(*Here shall enter the three Maries arrayed as chaste women,
with signs of the Passion[4] printed upon their breast, thus saying
Magdalene:*)

MARY MAGDALENE.   Alas, alas, for that royal
   beam!°   . *tree (i.e., the cross)*
Ah, this pierceth my heart worst of all;
For here he turned again to the woman of Jerusalem,   995
And for weariness let the cross fall.

---

1 *Limbo* In medieval cosmology, the borderlands of Hell, where the righteous dead such as Adam, Abraham, and Moses were kept imprisoned before the coming of Christ. Like the other prisoners of Hell, these are said to have been freed during the Harrowing.

2 *That ... wrack* That incredible deed did us harm.

3 *Friday at noon* The devil refers to Christ's death on Good Friday; since he then notes that Christ is risen, it is now Easter Sunday.

4 *signs of the Passion* Images of the instruments used to torture and crucify Christ: these would include such objects as the cross, nails, whips, spear, and crown of thorns. The Three Maries are wearing clothing with these images depicted upon them.

MARY JACOBE. This sorrow is bitterer than any gall,
    For here the Jews spurned° him to make him go,   *kicked*
    And they despited° their king royal.   *scorned*
1000   That cleaveth mine heart, and maketh me woe.

MARY SALOME. It is intolerable to see or to tell,
    For any creature, that strong tormentry.
    O Lord, thou haddest a marvelous° mell;°   *astonishing / strife*
    It is too hideous to descry.°   *describe*

(All the Maries, with one voice, say this following:)

1005 THE THREE MARIES. Hail, glorious cross! Thou bearest that Lord
      on high
    Which by thy might didst lowly bow down,
    Man's soul from all thralldom° to buy   *slavery*
    That evermore in pain should 'a° been bound,   *have*
    By record of David,[1] with mild steven:°   *voice*

1010   *Domine, inclina caelos tuos, et descende!*[2]

MARY MAGDALENE. Now to the monument let us go
    Whereas our Lord and Savior laid was,
    To anoint him, body and bone,
    To make amends for our trespass.°   *sins*

1015 MARY JACOBE. Who shall put down the lid of the monument
    That we may anoint his gracious wounds,
    With heart and mind to do our intent,
    With precious balms, this same stounds?°   *hour*
MARY SALOME. That blessed body within these bounds
1020   Here was laid, with rueful moans.
    Never creature was born upon grounds°   *earth*
    That might suffer so hideous a pain at once.

(Here shall appear two angels in white at the grave.)

---

1 *David* King of Israel, traditionally said to be the composer of the psalms.
2 *Domine ... et descende!* Latin: Lord, bow down your heavens and descend (Psalms
  143.5).

ANGEL 1.　Ye women present, dread you right naught;[1]
Jesus is risen, and is not here!
Lo, here is the place that he was in brought.　　　　　　　　1025
Go, say to his disciples and to Peter he shall appear.
ANGEL 2.　In Galilee, withouten any were,°　　　　　*doubt*
There shall ye see him, like as he said.
Go your way, and take comfort and cheer,
For that° he said shall not be delayed.　　　　　　*what* 1030

(*Here shall the Maries meet with Peter and John.*)

MARY MAGDALENE.　O, Peter and John! We be beguiled;
Our Lord's body is borne away!
I am a-feared it is defiled.
I am so careful,° I wot° not what to say.　　　*worried / know*
PETER.　Of these tidings greatly I dismay.　　　　　　1035
I will me thither hie[2] with all my might.
Now, Lord defend us as he best may!
Of the sepulcher we will have a sight.

JOHN.　Ah, mine inward soul, standing in distress,
The which of my body should have a guide,　　　　　　1040
For my Lord standing in heaviness,
When I remember his wounds wide!

PETER.　The sorrow and pain that he did dree°　　　*endure*
For our offense and abomination!
And also, I forsook him in his tormentry;　　　　　　1045
I took no heed to his teaching and exhortation.

(*Here Peter and John go to the sepulcher, and the Maries following.*)

PETER.　Ah, now I see and know the sooth.
But gracious Lord, be our protection!

1　*Ye women ... right naught*　You women here, do not be afraid in any way.
2　*I will me thither hie*　I will get myself there quickly.

Here is nothing left but a sudar[1] cloth,
1050   That of thy burying should make mention.
       JOHN.   I am afraid of wicked oppression.
       Where he is become,° it cannot be devised.°   *gone / imagined*
       But, he said after the third day he should have resurrection;
       Long before, this was promised.

1055   MARY MAGDALENE.   Alas, I may no longer abide,°   *stay*
       For dolor° and disease° that in my heart doth   *sorrow / distress*
           dwell.
       ANGEL 1.   Woman, woman, why weepest thou?
       Whom seekest thou with dolor thus?
       MARY MAGDALENE.   Ah, fain would I wit, and I wist how,[2]
1060   Who hath borne away my Lord Jesus!

       (*Hic aparuit Jesus.*[3])

       JESUS.   Woman, woman, why sayest thou?
       Whom seekest thou? Tell me this.
       MARY MAGDALENE.   Ah, good sir, tell me now
       If thou have borne away my Lord Jesus,

1065   For I have purposed° in each degree°   *intended / way*
       To have him with me, verily,°   *indeed*
       The which my special Lord hath be,°   *been*
       And I his lover, and cause will fie.°   *trust*

       JESUS.   O, O, Mary!

1070   MARY MAGDALENE.   Ah, gracious Master and Lord,
           you it is that I seek!
       Let me anoint you with these balms sweet!
       Lord, long hast thou hid thee from my spece,°   *appearance, image*
       But now will I kiss thou for my heart's boot!°   *benefit*

---

1   *sudar*   A sudarium is a facecloth; the word also refers to the cloth of Saint Veronica,
    who, according to medieval tradition, wiped Jesus's face during his procession to Calvary.
    The word here may indicate a prop that, like Veronica's cloth, bears an imprint of Jesus's
    face.
2   *Ah, fain ... wist how*   Ah, gladly would I know, if I knew how.
3   *Hic aparuit Jesus*   Latin: Here Jesus appears.

JESUS. Touch me not, Mary; I did not ascend
To my Father in Deity, and unto yours.   1075
But go, say to my brethren, I will pretend
To stey to my Father in Heavenly towers.[1]

MARY MAGDALENE. When I saw you first, Lord, verily
I weened° ye had been Simon the gardener.   *believed*
JESUS. So I am, forsooth, Mary;   1080
Man's heart is my garden here.
Therein I sow seeds of virtue all the year.
The foul weeds and vices I rend up by the root.
When that garden is watered with tears clear,
Then spring virtues, and smell full sweet.   1085

MARY MAGDALENE. O, thou dear-worthy emperor, thou high
    divine!
To me this is a joyful tiding
And unto all people that after us shall reign,
This knowledge of thy deity,
To all people that shall obtain   1090
And know this by possibility.
JESUS. I will show to sinners as I do to thee,
If they will with fervency of love me seek.
Be steadfast, and I shall ever with thee be,
And with all those that to me be meek.°   *humble* 1095

(*Here avoideth° Jesus suddenly, thus saying*   *exits*
Mary Magdelene:)

MARY MAGDALENE. O sisters, thus the high and noble
    influent° grace   *flowing, abundant*
Of my most blessed Lord Jesus, Jesus, Jesus!
He appeared unto me at the sepulcher there I was;
That hath relieved my woe, and mored° my bliss!   *increased*
It is innumerable to express   1100

---

1 *But go ... Heavenly towers* "But go, say to my brothers I will lay claim to ascend to
   my Father, in Heavenly towers." Jesus is here asserting his legal right as king to claim
   Heaven's throne.

Or for any tongue for to tell
Of my joy, how much it is,
So much my pains it doth excel!

MARY SALOME.   Now let us go to the city, to Our Lady dear,
1105   Her to show of his welfare.
And also to disciples, that we have seen here;
The more it shall rejoice them from care!

MARY JACOBE.   Now, sister Magdalene, with glad cheer;
So would that good Lord we might with him meet!
1110 JESUS.   To show desirous° hearts I am full near.   *willing*
Women, I appear to you and say *avete.*[1]

MARY SALOME.   Now, gracious Lord, of your
nimious° charity,   *exceedingly great*
With humble hearts to thy presence complain;
Grant us thy blessing of thy high deity,
1115   Ghostly° our souls for to sustain.   *spiritually*
JESUS.   All those been blessed that sore refrain.
We bless you, Father, and Son, and Holy Ghost,
All sorrow and care to constrain,
By our power of mights most,

1120   *In nomine Patris, et Filii, et Spiritus Sancti. Amen.*[2]

Go ye to my brethren, and say to them there
That they proceed and go into Galilee;
And there shall they see me, as I said before,
Bodily, with their carnal° eye.   *physical*

(*Here Jesus devoideth again.*)

1125 MARY MAGDALENE.   O thou glorious Lord of Heaven region,
Now blessed be thy high divinity
That ever thou tookest incarnation,

---

1   *avete* Latin: goodbye.
2   *In nomine ... Amen* Latin: In the name of the Father, and of the Son, and of the Holy
Spirit. Amen.

Thus for to visit thy poor servants three.
Thy will, gracious Lord, fulfilled shall be
As thou commandest us, in all thing.   1130
Our gracious brethren we will go see,
With them to say all our liking.°   *pleasure*

(*Here devoid all the three Maries. And the King of Marseilles shall
begin a sacrifice.*)

KING.   Now, lords and ladies of great apprize,°   *worth*
A matter to move you is in my memorial:°   *recollection*
This day to do a sacrifice   1135
With multitude of mirth before our gods all,

With prayers in especial before his presence,

Each creature with heart demure.

QUEEN.   To that lord courteous and kind,
Mahound, that is so mickle° of might;   *much* 1140
With minstrelsy° and mirth in mind,   *music*
Let us go offer in that high king's sight.

(*Here shall enter a Heathen Priest and his Boy.*)

HEATHEN PRIEST.   Now, my clerk Hawken, for love of me,
Look fast mine altar were arrayed.°   *prepared*
Go ring a bell, two or three.   1145
Lightly,° child; it be not delayed,   *quickly*
For here shall be a great solemnity.
Look, boy, thou do it with a braid!°   *haste*
CLERK.   What, master? Wouldst thou have thy leman°   *lover*
   to thy bed's side?
Thou shall abide till my service is said!¹   1150

---

1   *Thou shall abide ... is said*   The Clerk is saying his own prayers and rebuffs the Heathen
Priest for interrupting him.

HEATHEN PRIEST.   Boy, I say, by Saint Coppin,
  No such words to thee I spake.
  CLERK.   Whether thou did or not, the first journey shall be mine,
  For, by my faith, thou bearest Watt's pack.[1]

1155 But sir, my master, great Morel,
  Ye have so filled your belly with gruel
  That it groweth great as the Devil of Hell.
  Unshapely thou art to see.
  When women come to hear thy sermon,
1160 Prettily with them I can hucken,°   *haggle, bargain*
  With Kyrchon and fair Marion;
  They love me better than thee.

  I dare say, and° thou shouldst ride,   *if*
  Thy body is so great and wide
1165 That never horse may thee abide
  Except thou break his back asunder.
  HEATHEN PRIEST.   Ah, thou liest, boy, by the Devil of Hell!
  I pray God, Mahound mote° thee quell!°   *may / kill*
  I shall whip thee till thy ass shall bell!°   *ring*
1170 On thy ass come much wonder!

  CLERK.   A fart, master, and kiss my groin!
  The Devil of Hell was thy eme.°   *uncle*
  Lo, masters, of such a stock he came;
  This kindred is a-sprung late![2]
1175 HEATHEN PRIEST.   Mahound's blood, precious knave!
  Stripes° on thy ass thou shall have,   *whippings*
  And raps° on thy pate!°   *blows / head*

  (*Beat him.*)

  KING.   Now, priests and clerks of this temple clear,°   *pure*
  Your service to say, let me see.

---

1 *Boy, I say … Watt's pack*   "Saint Coppin" and "Watt's pack" are obscure. The sense is that
  the Heathen Priest denies he called for his lover; the Clerk replies that in any case he will
  get the first chance with her because the Heathen Priest is fat.

2 *A fart, master … late*   The Clerk is claiming, insultingly, that the Priest comes from a
  low-born family (indeed a diabolical one) which only recently has come up in the world.

HEATHEN PRIEST.   Ah! Sovereign lord, we shall do our
  devoir.°   *duty*   1180
Boy, a book anon° thou bring me!   *immediately*

Now, boy, to my altar I will me dress;
On shall my vestment° and mine   *ritual garment*
  array.°   *equipment*
CLERK.   Now then, the lesson I will express,°   *read aloud*
Like as longeth¹ for the service of this day: 1185

Lectio Mahoundis, viri fortissimi Sarasenorum:²
Glabriosum ad glumandum glumardinorum,
Gormondorum alocorum, stampatinantum cursorum,
Counthtes fulcatum, congruriandum tersorum,
Mursum malgorum, Mararagorum,   1190
Skartum sialporum, fartum cardicutorum,
Slaundri stroumppum, corbolcorum,
Sniguer snagoer werwolfforum,
Standgardum lamba beffettorum,
Stroutum stardi strangolcorum,   1195
Rigour dagour flapporum,
Castratum rati ribaldorum.
Hounds and hogs, in hedges and hills,
Snakes and toads mote be your bells!
Ragnel and Ruffin, and other, in the waves,   1200
Grant you grace to die on the gallows!

HEATHEN PRIEST.   Now, lords and ladies, less and more,
Kneel all down with good devotion.
Young and old, rich and poor,
Do your offering to Saint Mahound,   1205
And ye shall have great pardon
That longeth° to this holy place;   *belongs*
And receive ye shall my benison,°   *blessing*
And stand in Mahound's grace.

---

1 *Like as longeth* Such as is appropriate.
2 *Lectio … Sarasenorum* Latin: The lesson of Mahound, mightiest man of the Saracens.
   The remainder of the Clerk's speech after the first line is gibberish based loosely on Latin
   grammatical forms.

1210 KING.   Mahound, thou art of mights most,
         In my sight a glorious ghost.
         Thou comfortest me both in country and coast
         With thy wisdom and thy wit,
         For truly, lord, in thee is my trust.
1215   Good lord, let not my soul be lost!
         All my counsel° well thou wotest,°   *purposes / know*
         Here in thy presence as I sit.

         This bezant° of gold, rich and round,   *coin*
         I offer it for my lady and me,
1220   That thou mayest be our comfort in this stound.°   *time*
         Sweet Mahound, remember me!

    HEATHEN PRIEST.   Now, boy, I pray thee, let us have a song;
         Our service by note let us sing, I say.
         Cough up thy breast!¹ Stand not too long!
1225   Begin the office° of this day.   *ritual*
    CLERK.   I hum and I haste, I do that I may
         With merry tune the treble to sing.

         (*Sing both.*)

    HEATHEN PRIEST.   Hold up! The Devil mote thee affray,
         For all out of rule thou dost me bring.²

1230   But now, sir king, queen, and knight,
         Be merry in heart, everichon!°   *everyone*
         For here may ye see relics bright:
         Mahound's own neck bone!
         And ye shall see, ere° ever ye gon°   *before / go*
1235   Whatsoever you betide,°   *happens*
         And ye shall kiss all this holy bone,
         Mahound's own eyelid!
         Ye may have of this great store,°   *trust*

---

1   *Cough up thy breast!* Clear your throat!
2   *Hold up! ... me bring* Stop! May the Devil attack you, because you are throwing me off
     of the song.

And° ye knew the cause wherefore;°   *if / why*
It will make you blind forevermore,   1240
This same holy bead!¹

Lords and ladies, old and young,
Goliath so good to bliss may you bring;
Mahound the body and Dragon the dear,
With Belial² in bliss everlasting,   1245
That ye may there in joy sing
Before that comely king
That is our god in fere.°   *fellowship*

PILATE.   Now, ye sergeants seemly,° what say ye?   *dignified*
Ye be full witty° men in the law.   *knowledgeable* 1250
Of the death of Jesus I will advised be;
Our sovereign Caesar the sooth° must needs know.   *truth*

This Jesus was a man of great virtue,°   *power*
And many wonders in his time he wrought;
He was put to death by causes untrue,   1255
Which matter sticketh in my thought.
And ye know well how he was to the earth brought,
Watched with° knights of great array.°   *by / arms*
He is risen again, as before he taught,
And Joseph of Arimathea, he hath taken away.   1260

SERGEANT 1.   Sovereign judge, all this is sooth that ye say.
But all this must be cured by subtlety,°   *cunningly denied*
And say how his disciples stole him away;
And this shall be the answer, by the assent of me.
SERGEANT 2.   So it is most likely for to be.   1265
Your counsel is good and commendable;

---

1   *relics bright ... holy bead*   Devotion to relics—objects associated with a saint or with Jesus—was an important part of medieval religious culture; they were said to have not only spiritual but also physical healing properties. There was also a widespread trade in phony relics. Here, the relics of Mahound are stated to have harmful rather than curative properties.
2   *Goliath*   Giant and enemy of King David at 1 Samuel 17;   *Dragon*   May refer to the creature at Revelation 12.9;   *Belial*   Demon mentioned at 2 Corinthians 6.

So write him a pistle° of specialty,   *letter*
And that for us shall be most profitable.

PILATE.   Now, messenger, in haste hither° thou come!   *here*
1270   One message thou must, with our writing,
To the sovereign emperor of Rome.
But first thou shall go to Herod the king,
And say how that I send him knowing°   *information*
Of Christ's death, how it hath been wrought.°   *done*
1275   I charge° thee: make no letting°   *command / delay*
Till this letter to the emperor be brought.

MESSENGER.   My lord, in haste your message to speed
Unto those lords of royal renown,
Doubt ye not, my lord, it shall be done indeed.
1280   Now hence will I fast, out of this town.

(*Here goeth the messenger to Herod.*)

MESSENGER.   Hail, sovereign king under crown!
The princes of the law recommend to Your Highness,
And sendeth you tidings of Christ's Passion,
As in this writing doth express.

1285 HEROD.   Ah! By my troth, now am I full of bliss!
These be merry tidings that they have thus done;
Now, certes,° I am glad of this,   *certainly*
For now are we friends that afore° were fon.° *before / enemies*
Hold a reward, messenger, that thou were gone,
1290   And recommend me to my sovereign's grace.
Show him I will be as steadfast as stone,
Far and near, and in every place.

(*Here goeth the messenger to the emperor.*)

MESSENGER.   Hail be you, sovereign, sitting in solace!
Hail, worthy withouten peer!
1295 Hail, goodly to grant all grace!

Hail, emperor of the world, far and near!

Sovereign, and° it please your high empire,   *if*
I have brought you writing of great apprize°   *value*
Which shall be pleasing to your desire,
From Pilate, your high justice.   1300
He sent you word with lowly° intent;   *humble*
In every place he keepeth your commandment,
As he is bound by his office.

EMPEROR.   Ah, welcome, messenger of great pleasance!
The writing anon° let me see.   *immediately* 1305
My judges, anon give attendance
To understand what this writing may be,
Whether it be good, or any diversity,°   *adversity*
Or else not for mine avail;°   *help*
Declare me this in all the haste.   1310

PROVOST.   Sir, the sentence° we will discuss,°   *meaning / reveal*
And° it please your high excellence;   *if*
The intent of this epistle° is thus: *letter*
Pilate recommendeth to your presence,
And of a prophet is the sentence,   1315
Whose name was called Jesus.
He is put to death with violence
For he challenged° to be King of Jews.   *claimed*

Therefore he was crucified to dead,
And since° was buried, as they thought reason.   *afterwards* 1320
Also, he claimed himself Son of the Godhead!
The third night he was stolen away with treason,
With his disciples that to him had delection,°   *delight*
So with him away they yode.°   *went*
I marvel how they did with the body's corruption;° *decomposition* 1325
I trow they were fed with a froward food.[1]

---

1 *I trow … froward food* I believe that they were fed with an unpleasant food; i.e., that
they were rewarded with an unpleasant task.

EMPEROR.   Crafty was their cunning, the sooth° for to say.   *truth*
    This epistle I will keep with me if I can.
    Also I will have chronicled the year and the reign;
1330 That never shall be forgot, whoso look thereon.

    Messenger, out of this town with a rage;°   *haste*
    Hold° this gold to° thy wage,   *take (hold of) / for*
    Merry for to make!
  MESSENGER.   Farewell, my lord of great renown,
1335 For out of town my way I take.

(*Here enter Magdalene with her disciple, thus saying:*)

MARY MAGDALENE.   Ah, now I remember my Lord that put was
    to death
    With the Jews, withouten guilt or treason.
    The third night he rose by the might of his Godhead,
    Upon the Sunday had his glorious resurrection,
1340 And now is the time past of his glorious ascension;
    He steyed° to Heaven, and there he is king.   *ascended*
    Ah! His great kindness may not from my mention![1]
    Of all men's tongues he gave us knowing,

    For to understand every language.[2]
1345 Now have the disciples taken their passage
    To diverse countries here and yonder,
    To preach and teach of his high° damage.°   *noble / passion*
    Full far are my brethren departed asunder.

(*Here shall heaven open, and Jesus shall show.*)

JESUS.   O, the uneclipsed sun, temple of Solomon!
1350 In the moon I rested, that never changed goodness;
    In the ship of Noah; fleece of Gideon;
    She was my tabernacle of great nobleness;

---

1 *His great ... my mention* His great kindness cannot escape my mention.
2 *For to understand every language* Mary Magdalene refers here to Pentecost (Acts 2.1–
   31), in which the disciples gain this ability by divine intervention.

She was the palace of Phoebus'° brightness;   *the sun*
She was the vessel of pure cleanness
Where my Godhead gave my manhood might: 1355

My blessed mother, of demure femininity;
For mankind the fiend's defense;
Queen of Jerusalem, that Heavenly city;
Empress of Hell, to make resistance;
She is the precious pine full of incense;   1360
The precious cinnabar; the body through to seek;
She is the musk° against the heart of violence;   *ointment*
The gentle gillyflower against the cardiacle's wretch.[1]

The goodness of my mother no tongue can express,
Nor no clerk° of her, her joys can write.   *scholar* 1365
But now of my servant I remember the kindness;
With heavenly message I cast° me to visit.   *intend*
Raphael, mine angel in my sight,
To Mary Magdalene descend in a while.
Bid her pass the sea by my might,   1370
And say she shall convert the land of Marseilles.[2]

RAPHAEL.   O glorious Lord, I will resort°   *go*
To show your servant of your grace,
She shall labor for that land's comfort,
From heaviness them to purchase.   1375

(*Tunc descendet angelus.*[3])

RAPHAEL.   Abase° thee not, Mary, in this place!   *bow*
Our Lord's precept thou must fulfill:
To pass the sea in short space,
Unto the land of Marseilles.

---

1   *The gentle ... wretch*   The noble gillyflower, medicine for heart disease.
2   *Marseilles*   City on the southern (Mediterranean) coast of France; during the period of
    this play's composition it was a wealthy, powerful, and independent trading and military
    power. The story of Mary Magdalene's time in Marseilles was well known in the Middle
    Ages, recounted in such sources as Jacobus de Voragine's thirteenth-century *Legenda Au-
    rea* (Latin: Golden Legend).
3   *Tunc descendet angelus*   Latin: Then the angel descends.

1380 King and queen convert shall ye,
And be admitted as an holy apostless.
All the land shall be teached° alonely by thee;   *taught*
God's laws unto them ye shall express.
Therefore, haste you forth with gladness,
1385 God's commandment for to fulfill.

    MARY MAGDALENE.   He that from my person seven devils made
      to flee,
By virtue of him all thing was wrought;[1]
To seek those people I will ready° be.   *eager*
As thou hast commanded, in virtue° they shall be   *goodness*
  brought.

1390 With thy grace, good Lord in Deity,
Now to the sea I will me hie,°   *hurry*
Some shipping to espy.°   *find*
Now speed° me, Lord in eternal glory!   *help*
Now be my speed, Almighty Trinity!

    (*Here shall enter a ship with a merry song.*)

1395 SHIPMAN.   Strike! Strike! Let fall an anchor to ground!
    Here is a fair haven° to see.   *harbor*
    Cunningly in, look that ye sound!°   *test the water's depth*
    I hope good harbor have shall we;

    Look that we have drink, boy, thou!
1400 BOY.   I may not, for sleep,° I make God a vow;   *sleepiness*

    Thou shall abide° it, and° thou were my sire.°   *wait for / if / father*
    SHIPMAN.   Why, boy, we are ready to go to dinner;
    Shall we no meat° have?   *food*
    BOY.   Not for me. Be of good cheer,
1405 Though ye be sore hungered till ye rave,
I tell you plainly before.
For such a cramp on me set is,
I am at point to fare the worse.

---

1 *By virtue ... was wrought* By his power everything was made.

I lie and wring till I piss,
And am at point to be forlorn!   1410

SHIPMAN.   Now, boy, what will thee this sele?[1]
BOY.   Nothing but a fair damsel.
She should help me, I know it well,
Or else I may rue the time that I was born!
SHIPMAN.   Be my troth, sir boy, ye shall be sped!°   *helped* 1415
I will her bring unto your bed!
Now shall thou learn a damsel to wed;
She will not kiss thee, in scorn!

(*Beat him.*)

BOY.   Ah, scorn? No, no, I find it earnest!
The Devil of Hell mote° thee burst,   *may* 1420
For all my courage is now cast!°   *destroyed*
Alas, I am forlorn!

MARY MAGDALENE.   Master of the ship, a word with thee!
SHIPMAN.   All ready, fair woman! What will ye?
MARY MAGDALENE.   Of whence is this ship? Tell ye me,   1425
And if ye sail within a while.
SHIPMAN.   We will sail this same day,
If the wind be to our pay.°   *favor*
This ship that I of say,
Is of the land of Marseilles.   1430

MARY MAGDALENE.   Sir, may I not with you sail?
And ye shall have for your avail.°   *help*
SHIPMAN.   Of shipping ye shall not fail,
For us the wind is good and safe.
Yond° there is the land of Turkey;   *yonder* 1435
I were full loth for to lie!
Yonder is the land of Antalya;
Of this course we tharf° not abaft.°[2]   *need / go back (aft)*

---

1   *Now, boy ... this sele*   Now, boy, what do you want at this time?
2   *Yonder ... not abaft*   Lines 1437 and 1438 are reversed in the manuscript.

(*Now shall the shipmen sing.*)

SHIPMAN.   Strike! Beware of sand!
1440 Cast a lead, and in us guide!
Of Marseilles this is the king's land.
Go a-land,° thou fair woman, this tide,°   *ashore / time*
To the king's place. Yonder may ye see.

BOY.   Set off! Set off from land!
1445 All ready, master, at thine hand!

(*Here goeth the ship out of the place.*)

MARY MAGDALENE.   O Jesus, thy mellifluous name
Mote° be worshipped with reverence!   *may*
Lord, grant me victory against the fiend's° flame,   *devil's*
And in thy laws give this people credence!°   *belief*
1450 I will resort° by great convenience;°   *go / rightness*
In his presence I will draw near,
Of my Lord's laws to show the sentence,°   *meaning*
Both of his Godhead and of his power.

(*Here shall Mary enter before the king.*)

MARY MAGDALENE.   Now, the high king, Christ, man's
    redemption,
1455 Mote° save you, sir King, reigning in equity,   *may*
And mote guide you the way toward salvation.[1]
Jesus, the Son of the mighty Trinity,
That was, and is, and ever shall be
For man's soul the reformation,°   *restoration*
1460 In his name, lord, I beseech thee,
Within thy land to have my mansion.°   *home*

KING.   Jesus? Jesus? What devil is him, that?
I defy thee and thine opinion;
Thou false lurdan,° I shall fell° thee flat.   *villain / strike*
1465 Who made thee so hardy, to make such rebound?°   *reply*

---

1 *you the way ... salvation* The MS confusingly reads "you you the toward salvation."

MARY MAGDALENE.   Sir, I come not to thee for no deception;
 But that good Lord, Christ, hither° me compassed.°   *here / brought*
 To receive his name, it is your refection,°   *refreshment*
 And° thy form of misbelief by him may be loosed.   *if*

KING.   And what is that lord that thou speak of here?   1470
MARY MAGDALENE.   *Id est Salvator*,[1] if thou will lear,°   *learn*
 The Second Person, that Hell did conquer,

And the Son of the Father in Trinity!
KING.   And of what power is that God that ye
  rehearse° to me?   *declare*
MARY MAGDALENE.   He made Heaven and Earth, land and sea,   1475
 And all this he made of naught.
KING.   Woman, I pray° thee, answer me: *ask*
 What made God at the first beginning?
 This process, understand will we.
 That would I learn; it is my pleasing.°   *desire*   1480

MARY MAGDALENE.[2] Sir, I will declare all and sum,
 What from God first did proceed.
 He said, *In principio erat verbum*,[3]
 And with that he proved his great Godhead.
 He made Heaven for our speed,°   *help*   1485
 Whereas he sitteth in thrones high;
 His ministers next, as he saw need:
 His angels and archangels, all the company.

Upon the first day God made all this,
 As it was pleasing to his intent.   1490
 On the Monday, he would not miss°   *fail*
 To make sun, moon, and stars, and the firmament:

---

1   *Id est Salvator*   Latin: He is the Savior.
2   *MARY MAGDALENE*   The MS includes the phrase "Jesu mercy" at this point, which other
    editors have interpreted not as a line of dialogue but as a sign of scribal frustration. The
    scribe has, at this point, run out of room at the bottom of the leaf for the second page in
    a row, and is therefore required to split apart the speech attribution from the speech that
    follows it.
3   *In principio erat verbum*   Latin: In the beginning was the Word (John 1.1).

The sun to begin his course in the orient,°   *east*
And ever labor, withouten weariness,
1495   And keepeth his course into the occident.°   *west*

The Tuesday, as I understand this,
Great grace for us he gan° to increase.   *began*
That day he sat upon waters,
As was liking° to his goodness,   *pleasing*
1500   As Holy Writ beareth witness.
That time he made both sea and land,
All that work of great nobleness,
As it was pleasing to his gracious sond.°   *dispensation*

On the Wednesday, our Lord of might
1505   Made more at his pleasing:
Fish in flood, and fowl in flight,
And all this was for our helping.
On the Thursday, that noble king
Made diverse beasts, great and small.
1510   He gave them earth to their feeding
And bade them crease° by hill and dale.   *increase*

And on the Friday God made man
As it pleaseth his highness most:
After his own similitude° then,   *likeness*
1515   And gave them life of° the Holy Ghost.   *by means of*

On the Saturday, as I tell can,
All his works he gan° to bless.   *began*
He bade them multiply and increase then,
As it was pleasing to his worthiness.

1520   And on the Sunday he gan rest take,
As Scripture declareth plain,
That all should reverence make
To their maker that them doth sustain
Upon the Sunday to live in his service
1525   And him alonely to serve, I tell you plain.

KING.   Hark,° woman, thou hast many reasons great;   *listen*
        I think unto my gods appertaining° they be.   *belonging*

But° thou make me answer soon, I shall thee fret°   *unless / torment*
And cut the tongue out of thy head!

MARY MAGDALENE.   Sir, if I said amiss,° I will   *wrongly*   1530
   return° again.   *depart*
Leave° your encumbrance° of   *let go / burden*
   perturbation°   *annoyance*
And let me know what your gods be,
And how they may save us from tribulation.

KING.   Hence to the temple that we were,
And there shall thou see a solemn sight.   1535
Come on, all, both less and more,
This day to see my gods' might!

(*Here goeth the king with all his attendants to the temple.*)

KING.   Look now: what sayest thou by this sight?
How pleasantly they stand; see thou how?
Lord, I beseech thy great might,   1540
Speak to this Christian that here seest thou!
Speak, good lord, speak! See how I do bow?
Hark, thou priest, what meaneth all this?
What? Speak, good lord, speak! What aileth thee now?
Speak, as thou art boot° of all bliss!   *helper*   1545

HEATHEN PRIEST.   Lord, he will not speak while Christian here is.
MARY MAGDALENE.   Sir king, and° it please your   *if*
   gentleness,°   *nobility*
Give me license my prayers to make
Unto my God in Heaven-bliss,
Some miracle to show for your sake.   1550
KING.   Pray thy fill till thy knees ache.

MARY MAGDALENE.   *Dominus illuminatio mea; quem timebo?*
Dominus, protector vitae meae; a quo trepidabo?[1]

---

1 *Dominus illuminatio ... a quo trepidabo?* Latin: The Lord is my light; whom shall I fear?
The Lord is the protector of my life; of whom shall I be afraid? (Psalms 26.1).

(Here shall the mament° tremble and quake.)   *idol*

MARY MAGDALENE.   Now, Lord of lords, to thy blessed name
    sanctificate,°   *holy*
1555 Most meekly° my faith I recommend:°   *humbly / present*
    Put down the pride of maments violate!°   *corrupt*
    Lord, to thy lover thy goodness descend!
    Let not their pride to thy poustie° pretend,   *spiritual authority*
    Whereas° is rehearsed° thy high name, Jesus!   *where / repeated*
1560 Good Lord, my prayer I faithfully send;
    Lord, thy rightwiseness° here discuss!°   *righteousness / reveal*

(Here shall come a cloud from Heaven, and set the temple on a fire,
and the priest and the clerk shall sink.[1] And the king goeth home,
thus saying:)

KING.   Ah! Out! For anger I am thus deluded!
    I will bewreak° my cruel teen!°   *avenge / harm*
    Alas, within myself I am concluded.°   *overcome*
1565 Thou, woman, come hither° and wit° what I mean;   *here / know*
    My wife and I together many years have been
    And never might be conceived with child;
    If thou for this canst find a mean,°   *remedy*
    I will obey thy God, and to him be meek° and   *humble*
      mild.°   *agreeable*

1570 MARY MAGDALENE.   Now sir, since thou sayest so,
    To my Lord I pray with rightful boon.°   *request*
    Believe in him, and in no mo,°   *more*
    And I hope she shall be conceived soon.

KING.   Avoid, avoid!° I wax° all sick!   *get out / become*
1575 I will to bed this same tide!°   *time*
    I am so vexed with yon° snake,°   *this / head-cold*
    That hath near to death me dight!°   *brought*

---

1 *shall sink* The actors playing the Heathen Priest and the Clerk descend into the Hell-space through a trapdoor.

(*Here the king goeth to bed in haste, and Mary goeth into an old
lodge° without° the gate, thus saying:*)   *hut / outside*

MARY MAGDALENE.   Now, Christ, my creator,
   me conserve° and keep,°   *preserve / protect*
   That I be not confounded° with this raddour!°   *defeated / fear*
   For hunger and thirst, to thee I weep;   1580
   Lord, demean° me with measure!°   *treat / moderation*
   As thou savedst Daniel from the lions' rigor°   *harshness*
   By Habakkuk thy messenger, relieved with
     sustenance,°   *support*
   Good Lord, so help me and succor,
   Lord, as it is thy high pleasance.   1585

JESUS.   My grace shall grow, and down descend
   To Mary, my lover that to me doth call
   Her estate° for to amend.°   *situation / aid*
   She shall be relieved with sustenance corporal.°   *physical*
   Now angels, descend to her in especial,   1590
   And lead her to the prince's chamber right.
   Bid her ask of his good by ways pacifical,°   *peaceful*
   And go you before her with reverent light.

ANGEL 1.   Blessed Lord, in thy sight
   We descend unto Mary.   1595
ANGEL 2.   We descend from your bliss bright;
   Unto your commandment we apply.°   *attend*

(*Tunc descendit angelus. Primus dixit:*[1])

ANGEL 1.   Mary, our Lord will comfort you send.
   He bade to the king ye should take the way,
   Him to assay° if he will condescend,°   *test / yield* 1600
   As he is sleeping, him to assay.
ANGEL 2.   Bid° him relieve you to God's pay,°   *tell / benefit*
   And we shall go before you with solemn light;
   In a mantle of white shall be our array.
   The doors shall open against° us by right.   *before* 1605

---

1 *Tunc ... dixit* Latin: Then the angels descend. The first one said.

MARY MAGDALENE.   O gracious God, now I understand;
  This clothing of white is tokening° of   *symbolic*
    meekness.°   *humility*
  Now, gracious Lord, I will not wond°   *hesitate*
  Your precept to obey with lowliness.

  (*Here goeth Mary with the angels before her to the king's bed, with*
  lights bearing, thus saying Mary:)

1610 MARY MAGDALENE.   Thou froward° king,   *rebellious*
    troublous° and wood,°   *troublesome / mad*
  That hast at thy will all world's weal,°   *wealth*
  Depart° with me with some of thy good,°   *share / goods*
  That am in hunger, thirst, and chill.
  God hath thee sent warnings fell;°   *grim*
1615 I rede° thee, turn and amend° thy mood!°   *advise / change / heart*
  Beware of thy lewdness,° for thy own heal!°   *ignorance / health*
  And thou, queen, turn from thy good!°   *goods*

  (*Here Mary voideth° and the angel and Mary*   *exits*
  change her clothing, thus saying the king:)

  KING.   Ah, this day is come! I am merry and glad!
  The sun is up, and shineth bright!
1620 A marvelous showing° in my sleep I had,   *vision*
  That sore me troubled this same night:
  A fair woman I saw in my sight;
  All in white was she clad.
  Led she was with an angel bright;
1625 To me she spoke with words sad.°   *serious*

  QUEEN.   I trow° from God that they were sent.   *believe*
  In our hearts we may have doubt.°   *fear*
  I weened° our chamber should a° burnt,   *thought / have*
  For the light that there was all about.
1630 To us she spoke words of dread,
  That we should help them that have need
  With our goods, so God did bid,
  I tell you withouten doubt.

KING. Now, seemly° wife, ye say right well.   *dignified*
  Ah, Knight, anon,° withouten delay!   *immediately* 1635
  Now, as thou hast been true° as steel,   *reliable*
  Go, fetch that woman before me this day.
KNIGHT 5. My sovereign lord, I take the way;
  She shall come at your pleasance.
  Your sovereign will, I will go say;   1640
  It is alms° her to advance.°   *a good deed / help*

(*Tunc transit miles ad Mariam.*[1])

KNIGHT 5. Speed° well, good woman! I am to thee sent,   *succeed*
  You for to speak with the king.
MARY MAGDALENE. Gladly, sir, at his intent;
  I come at his own pleasing.   1645

(*Tunc transit Maria ad regem.*[2])

MARY MAGDALENE. The might and the power of the high Trinity,
  The wisdom of the Son, mote° govern you in right!   *may*
  The Holy Ghost mote with you be!
  What is your will? Say me in sight.
KING. Thou fair woman, it is my delight;   1650
  Thee to refresh is mine intent
  With meat,° and money, and clothes for the night,   *food*
  And with such grace as God hath me lent.

MARY MAGDALENE. Then fulfill ye God's commandment:
  Poor folk in mischief,° them to sustain.   *misfortune* 1655
KING. Now, blessed woman, rehearse° here present   *declare*
  The joys of your Lord in Heaven.

MARY. Ah, blessed the hour and blessed be the time
  That to God's laws ye will give credence.
  To yourself ye make a glad prime°   *beginning* 1660
  Against the fiend's malicious violence.

---

1 *Tunc ... Mariam* Latin: Then the knight crosses to Mary.
2 *Tunc ... regem* Latin: Then Mary crosses to the king.

From God above cometh the influence,
By the Holy Ghost, into thy breast sent down
For to restore° thy offence,   *redeem*
1665   Thy soul to bring to everlasting salvation.
Thy wife, she is great with child!
Like as thou desirest, thou hast thy boon.°   *wish*

QUEEN.   Ah, yea! I feel it stir in my womb up and down!
I am glad I have thee in presence;
1670   O blessed woman, root of our salvation,
Thy God will I worship with due reverence.

KING.   Now, fair woman, say me the sentence,°   *meaning*
I beseech thee: what is thy name?
MARY MAGDALENE.   Sir, against that I make no resistance;
1675   Mary Magdalene, withouten blame.[1]

KING.   O blessed Mary, right well is me,
That ever I have abided° this day.   *awaited*
Now thank I thy God, and specially thee,
And so shall I do while I live may.
1680 MARY MAGDALENE.   Ye shall thank Peter, my master, without
delay;
He is thy friend, steadfast and clear.°   *pure*
To Almighty God he helps me pray,
And he shall christen° you from the fiend's° power   *baptize / devil's*

In the sight of God on high.

1685 KING.   Now, surely ye answer me to my pay;°   *benefit*
I am right glad of these tidings.
But Mary, in all my goods I cease° you this day   *cede*
For to be at your guiding,
And them to rule at your pleasing
1690   Till that I come home again.
I will ask of you neither land nor reckoning,°   *accounting*
But I here deliver you power plain.°   *absolute*

---

1   *withouten blame*   A metrical tag meaning, "indeed."

QUEEN. Now, worshipful° lord, of a boon° *honorable / wish*
  I you pray,° *ask*
  And° it be pleasing to your high dignity. *if*
KING. Madam, your desire unto me say; 1695
  What boon is that ye desire of me?
QUEEN. Now, worshipful sovereign in each degree,° *way*
  That I may with you go
  A Christian woman made to be.
  Gracious lord, it may be so. 1700

KING. Alas, the wits of women, how they been wild;
  And thereof° falleth° many a chance!° *from that / happens / accident*
  Ah, why desire it you, and are with child?

QUEEN. Ah, my sovereign, I am knit in care,
  But° ye consider now that I crave, *unless* 1705
  For all the laws that ever were,
  Behind you that ye me not leave!

KING. Wife, since that ye will take this way° of *journey*
  price,° *value*
  Thereto can I no more say.
  Now Jesus be our guide, that is high justice,° *judge* 1710
  And this blessed woman, Mary Magdalene.

MARY MAGDALENE. Since ye are consented to that deed,
  The blessing of God give to you will I.
  He shall save you from all dread,
  In nomine Patris, et Filii, et Spiritus Sancti. Amen![1] 1715

(*Et tunc navis venit in plateam, et nauta dicit:*[2])

SHIPMAN. Look forth, Grub, my knave,° *servant*
  And tell me what tidings° thou have, *news*

---

1 *In nomine ... Amen!* Latin: In the name of the Father, and of the Son, and of the Holy Spirit. Amen!

2 *Et tunc navis ... nauta dicit* Latin: And then the ship comes into the place, and the sailor says.

And if thou espy° any land.   *see*

    Boy.   Into the shrouds° I will me hie.°   *rigging / hasten*

1720   By my faith, a castle I espy,

    And as I understand.

    Shipman.   Set° therewith,° if we maun,°   *land / therefore / can*

    For I wit° it is a haven-town°   *know / port*

    That standeth upon a strand.°   *shore*

    (*Et tunc transit rex ad navem, et dicit rex:*[1])

1725 King.   How, good man, of whence is that ship?

    I pray thee sir, tell thou me.

    Shipman.   Sir, as for that, I take no keep;°   *worry*

    For what cause inquire ye?

    King.   For causes of need, sail would we,

1730   Right fain° we would over° been.°   *gladly / overseas / be*

    Shipman.   Yea, but me thinketh, so mote I thee,

    So hastily to pass, your spending is thin.[2]

    I trow,° by my life,   *think*

    Thou hast stolen some man's wife;

1735   Thou wouldst lead her out of land.

    Nevertheless, so God me save,

    Let see what I shall have,[3]

    Or else I will not wend.°   *go*

    King.   Ten marks[4] I will thee give

1740   If thou wilt set me up[5] at the cliff

    In the Holy Land.

    Shipman.   Set off, boy, into the flood!°   *sea*

    Boy.   I shall, master. The wind is good;

    Hence that we were.[6]

---

1 *Et tunc ... dicit rex*   Latin: And then the king crosses to the ship, and the king says.

2 *Yea, but me ... is thin*   Yes, but as I may thrive, it seems to me your money is too little to travel so hastily.

3 *Let see what I shall have*   Let me see what you will pay me.

4 *mark*   A coin worth slightly less than a pound. Ten marks would have represented a substantial amount of money, perhaps $1,000–$2,000 US dollars today.

5 *If thou wilt set me up*   If you will put me ashore.

6 *Hence that we were*   One wishes that we were away; i.e., let's get going.

(*Lamentando regina:*[1])

QUEEN. Ah, lady, help in this need,   1745
That in this flood° we drench° not!   *sea / drown*
Ah, Mary, Mary, flower of womanhood!
O blessed lady, forget me not!

KING. Ah, my dear wife, no dread ye have;
But trust in Mary Magdalene,   1750
And she from perils shall us save.
To God for us she will pray.

QUEEN. Ah, dear husband, think on° me,   *of*
And save yourself as long as ye may,
For truly it will no otherwise be.   1755
Full sore my heart it maketh, this day.
Ah, the child that betwixt° my sides lay,   *between*
The which was conceived on me by right,
Alas, that woman's help is away!
A heavy departing is betwixt us in sight,   1760
For now depart we.
For default° of women[2] here in my need,   *lack*
Death my body maketh to spread.
Now, Mary Magdalene, my soul lead!
In manus tuas, Domine.[3]   1765

KING. Alas, my wife is dead!
Alas, this is a careful° chance!°   *sorrowful / event*
So shall my child, I am adread,°   *afraid*
And for default° of sustenance.°   *lack / nourishment*
Good Lord, thy grace grant to me!   1770
A child between us of increase,°   *offspring*
And it is motherless!
Help me, my sorrow for to release,
If thy will it be!

---

1   *Lamentando regina*   Latin: The queen, lamenting.
2   *default of women*   The Queen is lamenting the fact that there are no other women aboard ship to act as midwives.
3   *In manus tuas, Domine*   Latin: Into your hands, O Lord.

1775 SHIPMAN.   *Benedicite, benedicite!*[1]
   What weather may this be?
   Our mast will all asunder!°   *break in half*
BOY.   Master, I thereto lay mine ear[2]
   It is for this dead body that we bear;
1780 Cast her out,[3] or else we sink under!

(*Make ready for to cast her out.*)

KING.   Nay, for God's sake, do not so!
   And° ye will° her into the sea cast,°   *if / intend / throw*
   Gentle sirs, for my love, do—
   Yonder is a rock in the west—
1785 As lay her thereon all above,
   And my child her by.
SHIPMAN.   As thereto° I assent° well.   *for that / agree*
   And she were out of the vessel,
   All we should stand the more in heal,°   *safety*
1790 I say you, verily.°   *truly*

(*Tunc remigant ad montem. Et dicit rex:*[4])

KING.   Lie here, wife, and child thee by;
   Blessed Magdalene be her rede.°   *support*
   With tears weeping, and great cause why,
   I kiss you both in this stead.°   *place*
1795 Now will I pray to Mary mild
   To be their guide here.

(*Tunc remigant a monte. Et nauta dicit:*[5])

---

1 *Benedicite, benedicite*   Latin: Bless us. This is a common exclamation in Middle English
   literature; here, the Shipman uses it both as an expression of shock at the sudden storm
   and as a quick prayer of protection from it.
2 *I thereto lay mine ear*   I would bet my ear on it. The Boy believes that the voyage is now
   cursed because of the corpse aboard ship.
3 *Cast her out*   Throw her overboard.
4 *Tunc remigant ... dicit rex*   Latin: Then they row to the mound. And the king says.
5 *Tunc remigant ... nauta dicit*   Latin: Then they row from the mound. And the sailor
   says.

SHIPMAN. Pay now, sir, and go to land,
For here is the port gave,° I understand;   *agreed to*
Lay down my pay in my hand,
And belive,° go me from.   *quickly* 1800

KING. I grant thee, sir, so God me save.
Lo, here is all thy covenant;°   *agreed-upon price*
All ready thou shall it have,
And a mark more than thy grant.°   *price*

And thou, page,° for thy good obedience,   *servant* 1805
I give you, beside° your stint,°   *in addition to / portion*
Each of you a mark for your wage.
SHIPMAN. Now he that made both day and night,
He speed you in your right,
Well to go on your passage.   1810

PETER. Now all creatures upon mold°   *land*
That been of Christ's creation,
To worship Jesus they are behold,°   *obliged*
Nor never against him to make variation.°   *rebellion*

KING. Sir, faithfully I beseech° you this day,   *beg* 1815
Where Peter the apostle is, wit° would I.   *know*
PETER. It is I, sir. Without delay,
Of your asking, tell me why.

KING. Sir, the sooth° I shall you say,   *truth*
And tell you mine intent within a while.¹   1820
There is a woman hight° Mary Magdalene   *named*
That hither° hath labored° me out of Marseilles, *here / persuaded*
Unto the which woman I think no guile,°   *deceit*
And this pilgrimage caused me to take
(I will tell you more of the style)°   *story* 1825
For to christen° me from woe and wrack.°   *baptize / harm*

---

1 *within a while* Quickly.

PETER.   O, blessed be that time that ye are fall° to grace,   *come*
         And° ye will keep your belief after° my teaching   *if / according to*
         And alonely° forsake the fiend Satanas,·   *entirely*
1830   The commandments of God to have in keeping.
    KING.   Forsooth,° I believe in the Father, that is of all   *indeed*
         wielding,°   *power*
         And in the Son, Jesus Christ,
         Also in the Holy Ghost, his grace to us spreading.
         I believe in Christ's death, and his uprising.

1835 PETER.   Sir, then what ask ye?
    KING.   Holy father, baptism, for charity,
         Me to save in each degree
         From the fiend's bond.
    PETER.   In the name of the Trinity,
1840   With this water I baptize thee
         That thou mayst strong be,
         Against the fiend to stand.

         (*Tunc aspergit illum cum aqua.*[1])

    KING.   Ah, holy father, how my heart will be sore
         Of commandment and° ye declare not the   *if*
         sentence.°   *meaning*
1845 PETER.   Sir, daily ye shall labor, more and more,
         Till that ye have very° experience.°   *true / understanding*
         With me shall ye dwell, to have more eloquence,
         And go visit the stations by and by.[2]
         To Nazareth and Bethlehem go with diligence,
1850   And by your own inspection your faith to edify.°   *build up*

    KING.   Now, holy father, dear-worthy and dear,
         Mine intent now know ye.
         It is gone full two year
         That I came to you over the sea
1855   Christ's servant and yours to be,

---

1   *Tunc ... aqua*   Latin: Then he sprinkles him with water.
2   *And go ... and by*   And go visit the holy places in a short time.

And the law of him ever to fulfill.
Now will I home into my country.
Your pure blessing grant us till
That,[1] faithfully, I crave.°   *desire*
PETER. Now in the name of Jesu,   1860
Cum Patre et Sancto Spiritu,[2]
He keep° thee and save.   *protect*

(*Et tunc rex transit ad navem. Et dicit rex*:[3])

KING. Hold near, shipman, hold, hold!
BOY. Sir, yonder is one called after cold.[4]
SHIPMAN. Ah, sir! I ken° you of old;   *know* 1865
By my troth,° ye be welcome to me.   *faith*

KING. Now, gentle mariner, I thee pray,
Whatsoever that I pay,
In all the haste that ye may,
Help me over the sea.   1870

SHIPMAN. In good sooth° we been attendant.°   *faith / ready*
Gladly ye shall have your grant°   *wish*
Withouten any covenant.°   *bargaining*
Come in, in God's name!
Grub, boy, the wind is nor-west;   1875
Fast about the sail cast!
Rear up the sail in all the haste,
As well as thou can!

(*Et tunc navis venit adcirca plateam. Rex dicit*:[5])

KING. Master of the ship, cast forth your eye;
Me thinketh the rock I gin° to espy.   *begin* 1880
Gentle° master, thither° us guy;°   *noble / there / guide*
I shall quit° your meed.°   *pay / reward*

---

1   *Your pure ... That*   Give us your holy blessing in this regard.
2   *Cum ... Spiritu*   Latin: With the Father and the Holy Spirit.
3   *Et tunc ... dicit rex*   Latin: And then the king crosses to the ship. And the king says.
4   *Sir, yonder ... after cold*   Sir, there's somebody saying it's cold. The Boy, possibly deliberately, misstates what the King has said.
5   *Et tunc ... Rex dicit*   Latin: And then the ship goes around the place. The king says.

SHIPMAN.   In faith, it is the same stone
              That your wife lieth upon.
1885   Ye shall be there even° anon,°   *indeed / immediately*
              Verily° indeed.   *truly*

KING.   O thou mighty Lord of Heaven region,
              Yonder is my babe of mine own nature,°   *bloodline*
              Preserved and kept from all corruption!°   *decay*
1890   Blessed be that Lord, that thee doth succor!
              And my wife lieth here, fair and pure!
              Fair and clear is her color to see;
              Ah, good Lord, your grace with us indure,°   *strengthen*

              My wife's life for to illumine.
1895   Ah, blessed be that pure virgin;
              From grievous sleep she ginneth° revive!   *begins to*
              Ah, the sun of grace on us doth shine;
              Now, blessed be God, I see my wife alive!

QUEEN.   O Virgo salutata,[1] for our salvation!
1900   O pulchra et casta,[2] come of noble alliance!
              O almighty maiden, our souls' comfortation!
              O demure Magdalene, my body's sustenance!
              Thou hast wrapped us in weal° from all   *welfare*
                 variance°   *adversity*
              And led me with my lord into the Holy Land!
1905   I am baptized, as ye are, by Mary's guidance,
              Of Saint Peter's holy hand.

              I saw the blessed cross that Christ shed on his precious blood;
              His blessed sepulcher also saw I.
              Wherefore, good husband, be merry in mood,
1910   For I have gone the stations by and by.
              KING.   I thank it, Jesus, with heart on high!
              Now have I my wife and my child both.

---

1   O Virgo salutata   Latin: O pure Virgin.
2   O pulchra et casta   Latin: O beautiful and chaste one.

I thank it Magdalene, and Our Lady,
And ever shall do, withouten othe.°   *anything more*

(*Et tunc remigant a monte. Et nauta dicit*:[1])

SHIPMAN.   Now are ye past all peril;   1915
Here is the land of Marseilles.
Now go a-land, sir, when ye will,
I pray you for my sake.
KING.   God-a-mercy, gentle mariner;
Here is ten pounds of nobles[2] clear.   1920
And ever thy friend both far and near,
Christ save thee from woe and wrack.°   *harm*

(*Here goeth the ship out of the place. And Magdalene saith*:)

MARY MAGDALENE.   O dear friends, be in heart stable;
And, how dear Christ hath you both.[3]
Against God be nothing° variable;   *in no way* 1925
Think how he made all thing of naught.
Though you in poverty sometime be brought;
Yet be in charity both night and day,
For they been blessed that so be sooth,°   *loyal*
For *paupertas est donum Dei*.[4]   1930

God blesseth all those that be meek° and good,   *humble*
And he blesseth all those that weep for° sin.   *because of*
They be blessed that the hungry and the thirsty give food;
They be blessed that be merciful against° wretched men.   *to*
They be blessed that be destruction of sin: 1935
These be called the children of life,
Unto the which bliss bring both you and me

---

1   *Et tunc ... nauta dicit*   Latin: And then they row to the mound. And the sailor says.
2   *ten pounds of nobles*   Ten pounds' worth of nobles. A noble was a gold coin worth a third
     of a pound; the King has therefore given the Shipman thirty gold coins—a very large
     amount of money, equivalent to perhaps $9,000–$10,000 US dollars today.
3   *And, how ... you both*   And [be aware of] how much Christ values you both. There
     seems to be a word missing in this line.
4   *paupertas est donum Dei*   Latin: poverty is God's gift.

That for us died on the rood tree. Amen.

(*Here shall the king and the queen kneel down. Rex dicit:*[1])

KING.   Hail be thou, Mary; our Lord is with thee,
1940   The health of our souls and repast°   *refreshment*
      contemplative!°   *spiritual*
    Hail, tabernacle of the blessed Trinity!
    Hail, comfortable° succor for man and wife!   *comforting*

QUEEN.   Hail, thou chosen, and chaste of women alone;
    It passeth° my wit to tell thy nobleness!   *surpasses*
1945   Thou relievest me and my child on the rock of stone,
    And also saved us by thy high holiness.

MARY MAGDALENE.   Welcome home, prince and princess both!
    Welcome home, young prince of due° and right!   *legal title*
    Welcome home to your own heritage without
      othe,°   *anything more*
1950   And to all your people present in sight!
    Now are ye become God's own knight,
    For soul-health salve° did ye seek,   *medicine*
    In whom the Holy Ghost hath take residence
    And driven aside all the deception of wretch.°   *evil*
1955   And now have ye a knowledge of the sentence,°   *meaning*
    How ye shall come unto grace.
    But now, in your goods again° I do you cease;°   *in return / cede*
    I trust I have governed them to your heart's ease.
    Now will I labor° forth, God to please,   *go*
1960   More ghostly° strength me to purchase.°   *spiritual / attain*

KING.   O blessed Mary, to comprehend°   *accomplish*
    Our sweet succor, on us have pity!
QUEEN.   To depart from us why should ye pretend?°   *intend*
    O blessed lady, put us not to that poverty!

---

1 *Rex dicit* Latin: The king says.

MARY MAGDALENE. Of you and yours I will have remembrance,   1965
   And daily your bid-woman° for to be   *prayer-woman*
   That all wickedness from you may have deliverance,
   In quiet and rest that live may ye.

KING. Now then, your pure blessing grant us till.°   *to*
MARY MAGDALENE. The blessing of God mote° you   *may* 1970
   fulfill.

Ille vos benedicat, qui sine fine vivit et regnat.[1]

(*Here goeth Mary into the wilderness, thus saying rex:*[2])

KING. Ah, we may sigh, and weep also,
   That we have forgone° this lady free.°   *lost / generous*
   It bringeth my heart in care and woe,
   The which our guide and governor should a° been.   *have* 1975
QUEEN. That doth persuade° all my blee,°   *affect / complexion*
   That sweet cypress, that she would so.
   In me resteth° neither game° nor glee°   *remains / delight / joy*
   That she would from our presence go.

KING. Now, of her going I am nothing° glad,   *in no way* 1980
   But my lands to guide I must apply
   Like as *sancte*[3] Peter me bade.
   Churches in cities I will edify;°   *build*
   And whoso° against our faith will reply,°   *whoever / argue*
   I will punish such persons with perplexion.°   *torment* 1985
   Mahound and his laws, I defy!
   Ah, his pride out of my love shall have pollution,°   *desecration*
   And wholly unto Jesus I me betake.°   *commit*

(*Maria in erimo.*[4])

---

1   *Ille vos ... et regnat* Latin: May he bless you, he who lives and reigns without end.
2   *rex* Latin: the king.
3   *sancte* Latin: holy.
4   *Maria in erimo* Latin: Mary in the wilderness.

MARY MAGDALENE.   In this desert° abide°   *wilderness / remain*
      will we,
1990   My soul from sin for to save;
      I will ever abide me with humility,
      And put me in patience my Lord for to love.
      In charity my works I will grave°   *ground*
      And in abstinence, all days of my life.
1995   Thus my conscience of me doth crave;°   *demand*
      Then, why should I with° my conscience strive? *against*
      And furthermore, I will live in charity
      At the reverence of Our Blessed Lady,
      In goodness to be liberal,° my soul to   *generous*
        edify.°   *build up*
2000   Of worldly foods I will leave all refection;° *eating*
      By the food that cometh from Heaven on high
      That God will me send, by contemplative.° *spiritual power*

      JESUS.   O, the sweetness of prayers sent unto me
      From my well-beloved friend without variance.° *wavering*
2005   With ghostly° food relieved shall she be.   *spiritual*
      Angels, into the clouds ye do her hance;°   *lift*
      There, feed with manna[1] to her sustenance.
      With joy of angels, this let her receive.
      Bid her enjoy with all her affiance,°   *faith*
2010   For fiend's° fraud shall her none° deceive. *devil's / in no way*

      ANGEL 1.   O thou redolent° rose that of   *sweet-smelling*
        a virgin sprung!
      O thou precious palm° of victory!   *palm tree frond*
      O thou *hosanna*, angel's song!
      O precious gem, born of Our Lady!
2015   Lord, thy commandment we obey lowly;° *humbly*
      To thy servant that thou hast granted bliss,
      We angels all obey devoutly.
      We will descend to yon° wilderness.   *yonder*

---

1 *manna* The heavenly food that fed the Israelites in the desert (Exodus 16.31–35). Here
   it is identified with the obley, or Christian communion wafer.

(Here shall two angels descend into wilderness, and other two shall bring an obley,[1] openly appearing aloft in the clouds. The two beneath shall bring Mary and she shall receive the bread, and then go again into wilderness.)

ANGEL 2.   Mary, God greeteth thee with heavenly influence!
He hath sent thee grace with heavenly signs.   2020
Thou shall been° honored with joy and reverence,   *be*
Enhanced in Heaven above virgins.
Thou hast bigged° thee here among spines;°   *settled / thorns*
God will send thee food by revelation.
Thou shall be received into the clouds,   2025
Ghostly food to receive to thy salvation.

MARY MAGDALENE.   *Fiat voluntas tua*[2] in Heaven and Earth!
Now am I full of joy and bliss;
Laud and praise to that blessed birth!
I am ready, as his blessed will is.   2030

*(Here shall she be halsed° with angels with reverent   greeted
song. Assumpta est Maria in nubibus. Caeli gaudent, angeli
laudantes filium Dei. Et dicit Maria:[3])*

MARY MAGDALENE.   O thou Lord of lords, of high domination!
In Heaven and Earth worshipped be thy name.
How thou dividest° me from hunger and vexation;   *separate*
O glorious Lord, in thee is no fraud nor no defame!°   *dishonor*
But° I should serve my Lord, I were° to blame,   *unless / would be* 2035
Which fulfilleth me with so great felicity,°   *happiness*
With melody of angels showeth me glee° and   *joy*
   game,°   *delight*
And have fed me with food of most delicity!°   *delight*

(Here shall speak an holy priest in the same wilderness, thus saying the priest:)

---

1   *obley*   Communion wafer.
2   *Fiat voluntas tua*   Latin: Thy will be done (Matthew 6.10).
3   *Assumpta est ... dicit Maria*   Latin: Mary is taken up into the clouds. The heavens rejoice, the angels praising the Son of God. And Mary says.

PRIEST.   O Lord of lords, what may this be?
2040   So great mystery is showed from Heaven,
With great mirth and melody
With angels bright as the levin!°   *lightning*
Lord Jesus, for thy names seven,[1]
As grant me grace that person to see.

(*Here he shall go in the wilderness and spy°*   *see*
Mary in her devotion, thus saying the priest:)

2045   PRIEST.   Hail, creature,° Christ's delection!°   *created being / delight*
Hail, sweeter than sugar or cypress!
Mary is thy name, by angel's relation;°   *account*
Great art thou with God for thy perfectness!
The joy of Jerusalem showed thee express,°   *openly*
2050   The which I never saw this thirty winter and more;
Wherefore° I know well thou art of great perfectness.   *therefore*
I will pray you heartily to show me of your Lord.

MARY MAGDALENE.   By the grace of my Lord Jesus,
This thirty winter this hath been my cell,[2]
2055   And thrice on the day enhanced° thus,   *lifted up*
With more joy than any tongue can tell.
Never creature came there° I dwell,   *where*
Time nor tide, day nor night,
That I can with speech tell,
2060   But alonely with God's angels bright.[3]
But thou art welcome unto my sight,
If thou be of good conversation.[4]
As I think in my delight,
Thou shouldst° be a man of devotion.   *appear to*

---

1   *thy names seven*   Rabbinical traditions sometimes speak of the seven names of God; exactly how the phrase made its way into this medieval Christian play is somewhat uncertain.

2   *my cell*   My small room, as in a monastery.

3   *This thirty winter ... bright*   That is, Mary Magdalene has not interacted with another human being for thirty years, only with the angels that lift her into the clouds three times a day.

4   *If thou be of good conversation*   If you are a person who speaks of holy things.

PRIEST. In Christ's law I am sacred° a priest,   *consecrated* 2065
Ministered° by angels at my mass.   *assisted*
I sacre° the body of our Lord Jesus Christ, *consecrate*
And by that holy manna I live in soothfastness.° *truthfulness*
MARY MAGDALENE. Now I rejoice of your goodness;
But time is come that I shall ascend.   2070
PRIEST. I recommend me with all humbleness;
Unto my cell I will pretend.°   *go*

(*Here shall the priest go to his cell, thus saying Jesus:*)

JESUS. Now shall Mary have possession
By right inheritance: a crown to bear.
She shall be fetched to everlasting salvation, 2075
In joy to dwell withouten fere.°   *equal*
Now, angels, lightly° that ye were there;   *quickly*
Unto the priest's cell appear this tide.°   *time*
My body in form of bread that he bear,
Her for to housel,° bid him provide.   *administer* 2080

ANGEL I. O blessed Lord, we be ready
Your message to do, withouten treason.
ANGEL 2. To her I will go and make reporter,° *report*
How she shall come to your habitation.

(*Here shall two angels go to Mary and to the priest, thus saying the angels to the Priest:*)

ANGELS. Sir priest, God commandeth from Heaven region 2085
Ye shall go housel° his servant *administer the Eucharist to*
 express,°   *immediately*
And we with you shall take ministration° *provision*
To bear light before his body of worthiness.
PRIEST. Angels, with all humbleness,
In a vestment° I will me array,° *ritual garment / dress* 2090
To minister° my Lord of great highness; *serve*
Straight thereto I take the way.

(*In erimo.*[1])

ANGEL 2.   Mary, be glad, and in heart strong
    To receive the palm° of great victory.   *palm tree frond*
2095   This day ye shall be received with angels' song;
    Your soul shall depart from your body.

MARY MAGDALENE.   Ah, good Lord, I thank thee without
    variance!°   *hesitation*
    This day I am grounded all in goodness,
    With heart and body concluded° in   *completed*
    substance.°   *physical form*
2100   I thank thee, Lord, with spirit of perfectness!

(*Hic aparuit angelus, et presbiter cum Corpus Dominicum.*[2])

PRIEST.   Thou blessed woman, inure° in   *practiced*
    meekness,°   *humility*
    I have brought thee the bread of life to thy sight
    To make thee sure° from all distress,   *secure*
    Thy soul to bring to everlasting light.

2105 MARY MAGDALENE.   O thou mighty Lord of high majesty,
    This celestial° bread for to determine°   *heavenly / decide*
    This time to receive it in me,
    My soul therewith to illumine.

(*Here she receiveth it.*)

    I thank thee, Lord of ardent love!
2110   Now I know well I shall not oppress.°   *be defeated*
    Lord, let me see thy joys above;
    I recommend my soul unto thy bliss.
    Lord, open thy blessed gates!
    This earth at this time fervently I kiss.

---

1 *In erimo* Latin: In the wilderness.
2 *Hic aparuit ... Dominicum* Latin: Here the angel appears, and the priest with the Body
   of the Lord.

In manus tuas, Domine[1]—   2115
Lord, with thy grace me wis°—   *guide*
Commendo spiritum meum. Redimisti me,
Domine Deus veritatis.[2]

ANGEL 1.   Now receive we this soul, as reason is,
In Heaven to dwell us among.   2120
ANGEL 2.   Withouten end to be in bliss;
Now let us sing a merry song!

(*Gaudent in caelis.*[3])

PRIEST.   O good God, great is thy grace!
O Jesus, Jesus! Blessed be thy name!
Ah, Mary, Mary! Much is thy solace   2125
In Heaven-bliss, with glee and game![4]
Thy body will I cure° from all manner blame,°   *protect / defilement*
And I will pass° to the bishop of the city   *bring*
This body of Mary to bury by name,
With all reverence and solemnity.   2130

Sufferants° of this process,° thus endeth   *followers / performance*
    the sentence°   *meaning*
That we have played in your sight.
Almighty God most of magnificence
Mote° bring you to his bliss so bright,   *may*
In presence of that King!   2135
Now, friends, thus endeth this matter;
To bliss bring those that been here!
Now, clerks, with voices clear,
Te Deum laudamus[5] let us sing.

(*Explicit originale de Sancta Maria Magdalena.*[6])

---

1   *In manus tuas, Domine*   Latin: Into your hands, O Lord (Psalm 30.6).
2   *Commendo ... veritatis*   Latin: I commend my spirit. You have redeemed me, O Lord
      God of truth (Psalm 30.6).
3   *Gaudent in caelis*   Latin: They rejoice in Heaven.
4   *game*   The MS reads "name."
5   *Te Deum laudamus*   Latin: We praise you, O God.
6   *Explicit ... Magdalena*   Latin: The original of the play of Mary Magdalene ends here.

2140   If anything amiss° be,   *wrong*
           Blame cunning,° and not me.   *intelligence*
           I desire the readers to be my friend,
           If there be any amiss, that to amend.°[1]   *fix*

---

1 *If anything amiss ... to amend* This final quatrain is directed by either the playwright or, more probably, the scribe to the readers of the manuscript; it is almost certainly not intended to be played by the actors.

In Context

Source Material

As discussed in the introduction, the story material presented in *Mary Magdalene* goes well beyond what is presented in the Bible. Relevant Biblical texts are presented here in the Douay-Rheims version.

from the Douay-Rheims Bible, Mark 16; Luke 7; John 11; John 20

from MARK 16

1   And when the sabbath was past, Mary Magdalen, and Mary the mother of James, and Salome, bought sweet spices, that coming, they might anoint Jesus.

2   And very early in the morning, the first day of the week, they come to the sepulchre, the sun being now risen.

3   And they said one to another: Who shall roll us back the stone from the door of the sepulchre?

4   And looking, they saw the stone rolled back. For it was very great.

5   And entering into the sepulchre, they saw a young man sitting on the right side, clothed with a white robe: and they were astonished.

6   Who saith to them: Be not affrighted; you seek Jesus of Nazareth, who was crucified: he is risen, he is not here, behold the place where they laid him.

7   But go, tell his disciples and Peter that he goeth before you into Galilee; there you shall see him, as he told you.

8   But they going out, fled from the sepulchre. For a trembling and fear had seized them: and they said nothing to any man; for they were afraid.

9   But he rising early the first day of the week, appeared first to Mary Magdalen, out of whom he had cast seven devils. ...

...

36 And one of the Pharisees desired him to eat with him. And he went into the house of the Pharisee, and sat down to meat.[1]

37 And behold a woman that was in the city, a sinner, when she knew that he sat at meat in the Pharisee's house, brought an alabaster box of ointment;

38 And standing behind at his feet, she began to wash his feet, with tears, and wiped them with the hairs of her head, and kissed his feet, and anointed them with the ointment.

39 And the Pharisee, who had invited him, seeing it, spoke within himself, saying: This man, if he were a prophet, would know surely who and what manner of woman this is that toucheth him, that she is a sinner.

40 And Jesus answering, said to him: Simon, I have somewhat to say to thee. But he said: Master, say it.

41 A certain creditor had two debtors, the one who owed five hundred pence, and the other fifty.

42 And whereas they had not wherewith to pay, he forgave them both. Which therefore of the two loveth him most?

43 Simon answering, said: I suppose that he to whom he forgave most. And he said to him: Thou hast judged rightly.

44 And turning to the woman, he said unto Simon: Dost thou see this woman? I entered into thy house, thou gavest me no water for my feet; but she with tears hath washed my feet, and with her hairs hath wiped them.

45 Thou gavest me no kiss; but she, since she came in, hath not ceased to kiss my feet.

46 My head with oil thou didst not anoint; but she with ointment hath anointed my feet.

47 Wherefore I say to thee: Many sins are forgiven her, because she hath loved much. But to whom less is forgiven, he loveth less.

48 And he said to her: Thy sins are forgiven thee.

49 And they that sat at meat with him began to say within themselves: Who is this that forgiveth sins also?

---

1 *sat down to meat* In the sixteenth century "meat" was used to refer to a meal of any kind.

50 And he said to the woman: Thy faith hath made thee safe, go in peace.

from JOHN 11

1 Now there was a certain man sick, named Lazarus, of Bethania, of the town of Mary and Martha her sister.

2 (And Mary was she that anointed the Lord with ointment, and wiped his feet with her hair: whose brother Lazarus was sick.)

3 His sisters therefore sent to him, saying: Lord, behold, he whom thou lovest is sick.

4 And Jesus hearing it, said to them: This sickness is not unto death, but for the glory of God: that the Son of God may be glorified by it.

5 Now Jesus loved Martha, and her sister Mary, and Lazarus.

6 When he had heard therefore that he was sick, he still remained in the same place two days.

7 Then after that, he said to his disciples: Let us go into Judea again.

8 The disciples say to him: Rabbi, the Jews but now sought to stone thee: and goest thou thither again?

9 Jesus answered: Are there not twelve hours of the day? If a man walk in the day, he stumbleth not, because he seeth the light of this world:

10 But if he walk in the night, he stumbleth, because the light is not in him.

11 These things he said; and after that he said to them: Lazarus our friend sleepeth; but I go that I may awake him out of sleep.

12 His disciples therefore said: Lord, if he sleep, he shall do well.

13 But Jesus spoke of his death; and they thought that he spoke of the repose of sleep.

14 Then therefore Jesus said to them plainly: Lazarus is dead.

15 And I am glad, for your sakes, that I was not there, that you may believe: but let us go to him.

16 Thomas therefore, who is called Didymus, said to his fellow disciples: Let us also go, that we may die with him.

17 Jesus therefore came, and found that he had been four days already in the grave.

18 (Now Bethania was near Jerusalem, about fifteen furlongs[1] off.)

19 And many of the Jews were come to Martha and Mary, to comfort them concerning their brother.

20 Martha therefore, as soon as she heard that Jesus had come, went to meet him: but Mary sat at home.

21 Martha therefore said to Jesus: Lord, if thou hadst been here, my brother had not died.

22 But now also I know that whatsoever thou wilt ask of God, God will give it thee.

23 Jesus saith to her: Thy brother shall rise again.

24 Martha saith to him: I know that he shall rise again, in the resurrection at the last day.

25 Jesus said to her: I am the resurrection and the life: he that believeth in me, although he be dead, shall live:

26 And every one that liveth, and believeth in me, shall not die for ever. Believest thou this?

27 She saith to him: Yea, Lord, I have believed that thou art Christ the Son of the living God, who art come into this world.

28 And when she had said these things, she went, and called her sister Mary secretly, saying: The master is come, and calleth for thee.

29 She, as soon as she heard this, riseth quickly, and cometh to him.

30 For Jesus was not yet come into the town: but he was still in that place where Martha had met him.

31 The Jews therefore, who were with her in the house, and comforted her, when they saw Mary that she rose up speedily and went out, followed her, saying: She goeth to the grave to weep there.

32 When Mary therefore was come where Jesus was, seeing him, she fell down at his feet, and saith to him: Lord, if thou hadst been here, my brother had not died.

33 Jesus, therefore, when he saw her weeping, and the Jews that were come with her, weeping, groaned in the spirit, and troubled himself,

34 And said: Where have you laid him? They say to him: Lord, come and see.

---

1 *fifteen furlongs* A little under three miles.

35 And Jesus wept.

36 The Jews therefore said: Behold how he loved him.

37 But some of them said: Could not he that opened the eyes of the man born blind, have caused that this man should not die?

38 Jesus therefore again groaning in himself, cometh to the sepulchre. Now it was a cave; and a stone was laid over it.

39 Jesus saith: Take away the stone. Martha, the sister of him that was dead, saith to him: Lord, by this time he stinketh, for he is now of four days.

40 Jesus saith to her: Did not I say to thee, that if thou believe, thou shalt see the glory of God?

41 They took therefore the stone away. And Jesus lifting up his eyes said: Father, I give thee thanks that thou hast heard me.

42 And I knew that thou hearest me always; but because of the people who stand about have I said it, that they may believe that thou hast sent me.

43 When he had said these things, he cried with a loud voice: Lazarus, come forth.

44 And presently he that had been dead came forth, bound feet and hands with winding bands; and his face was bound about with a napkin. Jesus said to them: Loose him, and let him go.

...

from JOHN 20

...

11 But Mary stood at the sepulchre without, weeping. Now as she was weeping, she stooped down, and looked into the sepulchre,

12 And she saw two angels in white, sitting, one at the head, and one at the feet, where the body of Jesus had been laid.

13 They say to her: Woman, why weepest thou? She saith to them: Because they have taken away my Lord; and I know not where they have laid him.

14 When she had thus said, she turned herself back, and saw Jesus standing; and she knew not that it was Jesus.

15 Jesus saith to her: Woman, why weepest thou? whom seekest thou? She, thinking it was the gardener, saith to him: Sir, if thou hast taken him hence, tell me where thou hast laid him, and I will take him away.

16 Jesus saith to her: Mary. She turning, saith to him: Rabboni (which is to say, Master).

17 Jesus saith to her: Do not touch me, for I am not yet ascended to my Father. But go to my brethren, and say to them: I ascend to my Father and to your Father, to my God and your God.

18 Mary Magdalen cometh, and telleth the disciples: I have seen the Lord, and these things he said to me. ...

from Jacobus de Voragine, *Legenda Aurea* (*The Golden Legend*) (c. 1260)

> *The Golden Legend* was probably the most widely read compendium of saints' lives; close to 1,000 manuscript copies still survive. Compiled in the thirteenth century in Italy by a Dominican preacher (who later became an archbishop), the book was translated from the original Latin into all major European languages. William Caxton's English translation appeared in 1483; it was one of the first books he printed. Selections relevant to Mary Magdalene are included below, in the Caxton translation.

[Mary of Egypt]

Mary the Egyptian, which was called a sinner, led and lived the most straight life and sharp that might be, forty-seven years in desert. In that time was a good, holy and religious monk named Zosimus, and went through the desert which lieth beyond the flom¹ Jordan and much desired to find some holy fathers. And, when he came far and deep in the desert, he found a creature which was all black over all her body, of the great heat and burning of the sun, which went in that desert, and that was this Mary Egyptiaca aforesaid.

But as soon as she saw Zosimus come, she fled, and Zosimus after. And she tarried and said, "Abbot Zosimus, wherefore followest thou me? Have pity and mercy on me, for I dare not turn my face toward thee, because I am a woman and also naked, but cast thy mantle upon me, by which I may then, without shame, look and speak with thee."

---

1 *flom* River.

And when Zosimus heard himself named he was greatly a-marvelled, and anon he cast to her his mantle,[1] and humbly prayed her that she would give to him her blessing; and she answered, "It appertaineth to thee, fair father, to give the benediction, and nothing to me, for thou hast the dignity of priesthood."

...

"Fair father, I was born in Egypt, and when I was in the age of twelve years I went into Alexandria, and there I gave my body openly to sin by the space of seventeen years, and abandoned it to lechery and refused no man. After, it happed that men of that country went for to adore and worship the holy cross in Jerusalem, and I prayed to one of the mariners that he would suffer me to pass with the other people the sea, and when he me demanded payment for my passage, I answered, 'Fair sirs, I have nothing to pay you with, but I abandon my body to do withal your pleasure for my passage,' and they took me by that condition.

"And when I was come into Jerusalem unto the entry of the church for to worship the holy cross with the others, I was suddenly and invisibly put aback many times, in such wise that I might not enter into the church. And then I returned and thought in myself that this came to me for the great sins that I had committed in time past, and began to smite my breast and weep tenderly and sigh grievously. And I beheld there the image of our Lady, and I fell down and prayed her all weeping that she would impetre[2] and get me pardon of my sins of her sweet Son, and would suffer me to enter into the church for to worship the holy cross, promising to forsake the world, and from then forth on to live chaste... And after, I heard anon a voice: 'If thou wilt pass and go over flom Jordan thou shalt be safe,' and then I passed Jordan, and came into this desert, where I never saw man by the space of seventeen years...

"My clothes be rotten long sith,[3] and these seventeen first years I was much tempted by the burning of the sun much asprely,[4] and

---

1   *anon he cast to her his mantle*   At once he passed his cloak to her.
2   *impetre*   Beseech.
3   *sith*   Since.
4   *asprely*   Extremely.

many delectations that I have had in meat and drink, the good wines, and doing the desires of my body, all these came in my thought. Then I bewailed them on the earth, and prayed for help to our blessed Lady in whom I had set all my affiance, and I wept much tenderly. And anon I saw coming about me a great light, by the which I was all recomforted, and lost all the thoughts which oft and grievously tempted me. And sith, I have been delivered of all temptations and am nourished of spiritual meat of the word of our Lord. And thus have I been all my life as I have told to thee, and I pray thee by the incarnation of Jesu Christ that thou pray for me, sinful creature."

[Mary Magdalene]

Mary Magdalene had her surname of Magdalo, a castle, and was born of right noble lineage and parents, which were descended of the lineage of kings. And her father was named Cyrus, and her mother Eucharis. She with her brother Lazarus, and her sister Martha, possessed the castle of Magdalo, which is two miles from Nazareth, and Bethany, the castle which is nigh to Jerusalem, and also a great part of Jerusalem, which, all these things they departed among them. In such wise that Mary had the castle Magdalo, whereof she had her name Magdalene. And Lazarus had the part of the city of Jerusalem, and Martha had to her part Bethany. And when Mary gave herself to all delights of the body, and Lazarus entended all to knighthood,[1] Martha, which was wise, governed nobly her brother's part and also her sister's, and also her own, and administered to knights, and her servants, and to poor men, such necessities as they needed.

...

And when the blessed Mary Magdalene saw the people assembled at this temple for to do sacrifice to the idols, she arose up peaceably with a glad visage, a discreet tongue and well speaking, and began to preach the faith and law of Jesu Christ, and withdrew from the worshipping of the idols. Then were they a-marvelled of the beauty, of the reason, and of the fair speaking of her. And it was no marvel that

---

1 *entended all to knighthood* Attended all the time to his duties as a knight.

the mouth that had kissed the feet of our Lord so debonairly and so goodly, should be inspired with the word of God more than the other.

...

Then charged they a ship abundantly of all[1] that was necessary to them, and left all their things in the keeping of Mary Magdalene, and went forth on their pilgrimage. And when they had made their course, and sailed a day and a night, there arose a great tempest and orage.[2] And the wind increased and grew over hideous, in such wise that this lady, which was great, and nigh the time of her childing, began to wax feeble, and had great anguishes for the great waves and troubling of the sea, and soon after began to travail, and was delivered of a fair son, by occasion of the storm and tempest, and in her childing died....

And when he came to Saint Peter, Saint Peter came against him, and when he saw the sign of the cross upon his shoulder, he demanded him what he was, and wherefore he came, and he told to him all by order. To whom Peter said, "Peace be to thee, thou art welcome, and hast believed good counsel. And be thou not heavy if thy wife sleep, and the little child rest with her, for our Lord is almighty for to give to whom he will, and to take away that he hath given, and to re-establish and give again that he hath taken, and to turn all heaviness and weeping into joy." Then Peter led him into Jerusalem, and showed to him all the places where Jesu Christ preached and did miracles, and the place where he suffered death, and where he ascended into heaven.

And when he was well-informed of Saint Peter in the faith, and that two years were passed sith he departed from Marseilles, he took his ship for to return again into his country. And as they sailed by the sea, they came, by the ordinance of God, by the rock where the body of his wife was left, and his son. Then by prayers and gifts he did so much that they arrived thereon. And the little child, whom Mary Magdalene had kept, went oft sithes to the seaside, and, like small children, took small stones and threw them into the sea. And when they came they saw the little child playing with stones on the seaside, as he was wont to do. And then they marvelled much what he was.

---

1   *charged ... abundantly of all*   They supplied a ship fully with everything.
2   *orage*   Storm.

And when the child saw them, which never had seen people tofore, he was afraid, and ran secretly to his mother's breast and hid him under the mantle. And then the father of the child went for to see more appertly,[1] and took the mantle, and found the child, which was right fair, sucking his mother's breast.

Then he took the child in his arms and said, "O blessed Mary Magdalene, I were well happy and blessed if my wife were now alive, and might live, and come again with me into my country. I know verily and believe that thou who hast given to me my son, and hast fed and kept him two years in this rock, mayst well re-establish his mother to her first health." And with these words the woman respired, and took life, and said, like as she had been waked of her sleep, "O blessed Mary Magdalene, thou art of great merit and glorious, for in the pains of my deliverance thou wert my midwife, and in all my necessities thou hast accomplished to me the service of a chamberer."

And when her husband heard that thing he a-marvelled much, and said: "Livest thou, my right dear and best beloved wife?" To whom she said, "Yea, certainly I live, and am now first come from the pilgrimage from whence thou art come, and all in like wise as Saint Peter led thee in Jerusalem, and showed to thee all the places where our Lord suffered death, was buried and ascended to heaven, and many other places, I was with you, with Mary Magdalene, which led and accompanied me, and showed to me all the places which I well remember and have in mind." And there recounted to him all the miracles that her husband had seen, and never failed of one article, ne went out of the way from the sooth.[2]

...

In this meanwhile the blessed Mary Magdalene, desirous of sovereign contemplation, sought a right sharp[3] desert, and took a place which was ordained by the angel of God, and abode there by the space of thirty years without knowledge of anybody. In which place she had no comfort of running water, ne solace of trees, ne of herbs. And that was because our Redeemer did do show it openly, that he had

---

1   *appertly*   Clearly; openly.
2   *ne went ... from the sooth*   Nor departed in any way from the truth.
3   *right sharp*   Truly harsh; severe.

ordained for her refection celestial, and no bodily meats. And every day at every hour canonical she was lifted up in the air of angels, and heard the glorious song of the heavenly companies with her bodily ears. Of which she was fed and filled with right sweet meats, and then was brought again by the angels unto her proper place, in such wise as she had no need of corporal nourishing.

It happed that a priest, which desired to lead a solitary life, took a cell for himself a twelve-furlong from the place of Mary Magdalene. On a day our Lord opened the eyes of that priest, and he saw with his bodily eyes in what manner the angels descended into the place where the blessed Magdalene dwelt, and how they lifted her in the air, and after by the space of an hour brought her again with divine praisings to the same place.

And then the priest desired greatly to know the truth of this marvellous vision, and made his prayers to Almighty God, and went with great devotion unto the place. And when he approached nigh to it a stone's cast, his thighs began to swell and wax feeble, and his entrails began within him to lack breath and sigh for fear. And as soon as he returned he had his thighs all whole, and ready for to go. And when he enforced him to go to the place, all his body was in languor, and might not move.

And then he understood that it was a secret celestial place where no man human might come, and then he called the name of Jesu, and said, "I conjure thee by our Lord, that if thou be a man or other creature reasonable, that dwellest in this cave, that thou answer me, and tell me the truth of thee." And when he had said this three times, the blessed Mary Magdalene answered, "Come more near, and thou shalt know that thou desirest."

And then he came trembling unto the half way, and she said to him, "Rememberest thou not of the gospel of Mary Magdalene, the renowned sinful woman, which washed the feet of our Saviour with her tears, and dried them with the hair of her head, and desired to have forgiveness of her sins?" And the priest said to her, "I remember it well; that is more than thirty years that holy church believeth and confesseth that it was done." And then she said, "I am she that by the space of thirty years have been here without witting of any person, and like as it was suffered to thee yesterday to see me, in like wise I am every day lift up by the hands of the angels into the air, and have deserved to hear with my bodily ears the right sweet song of the company celestial. And because it is showed to me of our Lord that I shall depart out of this world, go to Maximin, and say to him that the next day after the resurrection of our lord, in the same time that he is accustomed to arise and go to matins, that he alone enter into his oratory, and that by the ministry and service of angels he shall find me there."

And the priest heard the voice of her, like as it had been the voice of an angel, but he saw nothing; and then anon he went to Saint Maximin, and told to him all by order. Then Saint Maximin was replenished of great joy, and thanked greatly our Lord. And on the said day and hour, as is aforesaid, he entered into his oratory, and saw the blessed Mary Magdalene standing in the quire or choir yet among the angels that brought her, and was lift up from the earth the space of two or three cubits. And praying to our Lord she held up her hands, and when Saint Maximin saw her, he was afraid to approach to her.

And she returned to him, and said, "Come hither, mine own father, and flee not thy daughter." And when he approached and came to her, as it is read in the books of the said Saint Maximin, for the customable¹ vision that she had of angels every day, the cheer and visage of her shone as clear as it had been the rays of the sun. And then all the clerks and the priests aforesaid were called, and Mary Magdalene received the body and blood of our Lord of the hands of the bishop with great abundance of tears, and after, she stretched her body tofore the altar, and her right blessed soul departed from the body and went to our Lord. And after it was departed, there issued out of the body an odour so sweet-smelling that it remained there by the space of seven days to all them that entered in. And the blessed Maximin anointed the body of her with divers precious ointments, and buried it honourably, and after commanded that his body should be buried by hers after his death.

---

1   *customable*   Customary.

The Manuscript

The following are two pages from Digby MS 133, followed by transcriptions into modern typography. The first page represents the beginning of the play, in which the Emperor begins his boast; the second represents the raising of Lazarus by Jesus and the transition to the King of Marseilles. The manuscript pages generally lack punctuation, and make use of abbreviations for common words such as "the," "your," "with," and "and." Syllables within words such as "er" and "ys" are also sometimes indicated with abbreviations, as are letters such as "m" and "n." The manuscript uses "x" to represent the sound that Modern English renders "sh," in common with other East Anglian texts. Additionally, some parts of the manuscript indicate non-spoken text such as speech attributions in different-colored ink; in the case of the second page given, they are written in red. Finally, some letters and words are crossed or blotted out in the manuscript and replaced by the scribe's own corrections, while some words are added above the main line due to shortage of space.

In the transcription, I have expanded abbreviations using italics; manuscript text in red ink is indicated with boldface. The scribe often uses horizontal lines across the page to divide speeches, characters, and stage directions; I have maintained these. Words appearing above the line are preceded in the transcription by a caret (^), and words and letters crossed out are placed between square brackets. Obsolete letters such as thorn and yogh have been replaced with their modern equivalents, and I have similarly replaced initial x with sh. The pages also contain later markings: the first page shows, at the top, the initials M B (for Myles Blomefylde, at one time an owner of the manuscript), and both pages show later numbering in the top right corner. Because these are later additions and not part of the original text, I have not transcribed them.

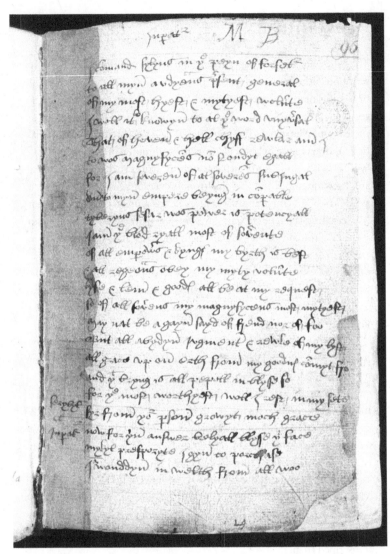

Mystery Play of St. Mary Magdalene. MS Digby 133, Folio 95r. The Bodleian Libraries. Reprinted with permission.

Imp*era*tor

I com*m*and sylyns in *the* peyn of forfet*ur*
to all myn avdyeans p*re*sent general
of my most hyest *and* mytyest wolu*n*te
I woll it ^be knowyn to al *the* word vnyv*er*sal
That of heven *and* hell chyff rewler am I
to wos magnyfyce*n*s no*n* stondyt egall
for I am soveren of al sovere*n*s subjugal
onto myn empere beyng in co*m*pa*r*able
tyberyus sesar wos power is potencyall
I am *the* blod ryall most of sov*er*ente
of all emp*er*owers *and* kyngs my byrth is best
and all regeou*n*s obey my myty volu*n*te
lyfe *and* lem *and* good*s* all be at my request
so of all sov*er*ens my magnyfycens most mytyest
may not be agayn sayd of frend nor of foo
But all abydyn jvgment *and* rewle of my lyst
all gras up on erth from my goodnes co*m*myt fro
and *that* bryngis all pepell in blysse so
for *the* most worthyest woll I rest in my sete
Serybyl————————————————————
Syr from y*our* p*er*son growyt moch grace
Imp*era*tor————————————————
now for *thin* answer belyall blysse *thi* face
mykyl presporyte I gyn to porc[c]hase
I ^*am* wounddyn in welth from all woo

Mystery Play of St. Mary Magdalene. MS Digby 133, Folio 116r. The Bodleian Libraries. Reprinted with permission.

Folio 116r; this corresponds to lines 910-924 s.d.

Lazar Lazar com hethy*r* to me

_____

Here shall lazar aryse trossyd *with* towells in a shete

Lazar

A my makar my savyou*r* blyssyd mott th*ou* be
here me*n* may know *thi* werk*ys* of won[b]dyr
Lord no thyng ys on possybyll to the
for my body *and* my sowle was dep*ar*tyd asond*er*
I shuld a rottytt as doth *the* tondyr
fleysch from *the* bonys aco*n*sumyd a[was]way
now is a loft *that* late was ondyr
the goodnesse of god hath don for me dere
for he is bote of all balys to on bynd
that blyssyd lord *that* here ded apere

_____

here all *the* pepull *and the* jewys mari & martha *with* on
woys sey thes word*ys* we be leve in yow savyow*r* ih*esus* ^ih*esus*
   ih*esus*

_____

Of [ow*er*] yow*er* good herty*s* I have ad v*er*tacyoun*ys*
where thorow in sowle holl made ye be
be twyx yow *and* me be nev*er* varyacyoun*ys*
Wherfor I say vade In pace

_____

here devoydyt ih*esus with* hy*s* desypull*ys* mary *and* martha
***and* Lazar*e* gon hom to *the* castell & here be gynnyt**
hys bost

From the Publisher

A name never says it all, but the word "Broadview" expresses a good deal of the philosophy behind our company. We are open to a broad range of academic approaches and political viewpoints. We pay attention to the broad impact book publishing and book printing has in the wider world; we began using recycled stock more than a decade ago, and for some years now we have used 100% recycled paper for most titles. Our publishing program is internationally oriented and broad-ranging. Our individual titles often appeal to a broad readership too; many are of interest as much to general readers as to academics and students.

Founded in 1985, Broadview remains a fully independent company owned by its shareholders—not an imprint or subsidiary of a larger multinational.

For the most accurate information on our books (including information on pricing, editions, and formats) please visit our website at www.broadviewpress.com. Our print books and ebooks are also available for sale on our site.

broadview press
www.broadviewpress.com

This book is made of paper from well-managed FSC® - certified forests, recycled materials, and other controlled sources.